Not Quite Je

A Play

Paul Kember

Samuel French – London
New York – Sydney – Toronto – Hollywood

NOT QUITE JERUSALEM

First presented by the English Stage Company at the Royal Court Theatre, London, on 2nd December, 1980, with the following cast of characters:

Dave	Bernard Strother
Mike	Philip Davis
Carrie	Annie Hayes
Pete	Kevin McNally
Ami	Bruce Alexander
Gila	Leslee Udwin

Subsequently revived in this revised version at the Royal Court Theatre, London, on 19th April, 1982, with the following cast of characters:

Dave	David Fielder
Mike	David Threlfall
Carrie	Selina Cadell
Pete	Kevin McNally
Ami	Bruce Alexander
Gila	Leslee Udwin

Directed by Les Waters
Designed by Peter Hartwell
The action of the play takes place in a kibbutz during spring and early summer

ACT I
  SCENE 1   The culture hall/dining-room at dawn
  SCENE 2   The refet (cowshed), a week later, early morning

ACT II
  SCENE 1   The swimming-pool, a month later, late afternoon
  SCENE 2   The culture hall/dining-room, a few days later, evening
  SCENE 3   The same, later the following evening

Time—the present

NOTE

Several lines of dialogue spoken by Gila and Ami are in Hebrew. Where this occurs an English translation is provided immediately after the Hebrew but only the Hebrew should be spoken.

ACT I

The kibbutz culture hall/dining-room. A spring morning at about 4 a.m.

There is a door DR which leads to the outside of the building and upstage of it a window, with another window on the opposite side wall. A second door, UL, leads to the rest of the rooms. On the upstage wall is a small curtained "stage" C, across which the curtains are drawn, and in front of it a tea trolley with a tea urn, cups, milk and sandwiches. R of the "stage" is a noticeboard and wall-telephone. The furniture is functional and minimal consisting of a table and three chairs ̇< and a fourth chair against the wall DL

Outside it is pouring with rain and quite dark although dawn is just breaking. Two Volunteers from England have just arrived for a working holiday and they are soaking wet, tired and despondent. One is Dave, from Yorkshire, and the other is Mike who is apparently flaked out, seated at the table, head in hands and half asleep. Both are in their mid-twenties. Dave's bag stands against the chair DL and Mike's suitcase and bag are on the table

Dave Hey, Mick.

Mike Yes, Dave? What now?

Dave Reckon we've made· a dreadful mistake? (*Pause*) Dismal, isn't it? (*Pause*) Bit like a fucking prison camp. Eh? (*Pause*) Your case is ruined. That cunt could have stopped, couldn't he? I told him to take the gear inside. Pretending he couldn't hear through the partition. Twat. He knew it'd get soaked.

An Alsatian dog barks, off

Where are these bleeding towels, then? I'm soaked to the skin. (*Pause*) Trust me, eh? Only I could get on a plane, travel two thousand miles in search of the sun, step off the plane— and get pissed on. (*Pause*) I'm gonna love this place. I can feel it.

The sound of a jeep approaching and stopping

This must be the others. I saw a blonde tart getting in the other jeep. Let's hope she's Swedish, eh?

Dave takes a comb from his pocket and combs his hair furiously

Carrie enters DR followed by Pete. She is a rather serious young woman, in mid to late twenties, wearing a raincoat, with hood up, and with a haversack on her back. He is in his twenties, has a haversack and is carrying Carrie's folding easel, large sketchpad and paints tied together

Carrie Dear God, I thought we were going to be shot. (*She removes her hood*)

Pete Tight security. Has to be. Siege environment. Did you notice the gun turrets? And the fence? Lecky, I reckon. Probably about twenty-three volts. Where do you want this?

Carrie Oh, I'll take it. Thanks ever so.

Carrie takes the easel, pad and paints and leans them against the "stage". She takes off her haversack and removes her coat. Pete puts his bag on the "stage" and moves over to Dave

Pete You speak English?

Dave English? Gummersal.

Pete Ah—Gummersal. (*He shakes Dave's hand. In a very pronounced voice*) Where are you from then?

Dave I just fucking told you. Gummersal—Yorkshire.

Pete Oh, fuck me. Yorkshire. Why didn't you say so? Where's he from?

Dave Dunno. Where you from, Mick?

Mike appears to be asleep

Clapped out. He's been like that all the way. Where you from?

Pete Harlow.

Dave (*whispering*) She English, too?

Carrie crosses to Pete and Dave carrying her coat and haversack

Carrie Yes, I'm English too.

Pete Nothing like travel for broadening the mind is there? You two come together then?

Dave No, we was sitting on the plane together, you know, got talking.

Carrie What's the accommodation situation like? Does anybody know?

Pete Three to a room, I heard.

Carrie moves the chair away from the wall DL, puts her coat on the back of it, and sits down. She takes off her shoes, takes a towel from her haversack and dries her feet. She puts on dry shoes from her haversack

Dave All I want is a bleeding towel, mate. That's all I'm worried about. Where is that geezer? I'm soaking.

Pete We were lucky. Ours was covered.

Dave How long was you waiting around, then?

Pete Oh, I had it all arranged, me. I came over a couple of days ago to do a bit of sightseeing in Tel Aviv. That took a good half-hour. Went to the kibbutz office. They told me to go to Ben Gurion airport at midnight and I'd meet a guy by the tea-stall. So I'm looking round for a guy by the tea-stall. Needless to say he didn't turn up. Or if he did, I didn't find him.

Dave That's the problem with Jew boys though, isn't it? They all look alike.

Pete Yeh, so I'm hanging round the airport like a spare prick asking everyone if they're from this kibbutz Sharr Ha'a . . . Shaar Ha'ama . . . something unpronounceable, and eventually I bumps into the guy from this place. He said they was looking for people and did I fancy picking water melons, so I thought, sod it, why not.

Dave We must have been quite lucky, then. We'd just stepped off the plane.

Carrie Can you smell the flowers? Isn't it amazing? It was just like that at the airport. That was the first thing I noticed when I got off the plane—the incredible, overpowering smell of flowers. In an airport. One expects the stench of gasoline, doesn't one?

Pete and Dave look at each other. Mike now sits up. An Alsatian is heard barking, closer than before

Why do they have to have Alsatians all over the place? I find them terrifying.

Pete What would you prefer for guard dogs—poodles?

Carrie They look so fierce.

Dave Yeah. Horrible bark. Woof! Woof!

Carrie Oh, please. My nerves.

Dave and Pete laugh. Dave crosses to the table

Dave Hey, Mick. At least we wasn't blown up in mid-air.

Mike We've got your St Christopher medal to thank for that, Dave.

Dave Right. (*He thinks about it*) Oh, you cunt.

Pete crosses to the table

Pete Weird, wasn't it, the roads, coming down here? Signposts in English. Hebrew, Arabic and English. They're even got roundabouts. Same as ours And office blocks. And orange street lamps. Can you imagine it? In the land where Jesus was born and bred, orange street lamps? It's just like home.

Dave Except for the tanks. No tanks in Gummersal.

Mike The year's not over yet, Dave.

Carrie The heat. Gracious.

Pete Humidity. That's what knackers you. Not the heat.

Carrie I wonder where we are? It's in the Negev desert, I know that.

Pete Near the sea. That's what accounts for the humidity.

Mike rises, crosses to the tea urn and takes a sandwich. Carrie gets up and moves away from her chair, her back to the door UL

Dave Where's these fucking towels?

Mike Tea's up.

Carrie Nobody said we could help ourselves.

Mike I'm sure I would have remembered if they had.

Pete and Dave move over to the trolley. Pete takes a sandwich and pours himself some tea

Dave What's this? I thought they'd lay on a meal. Sandwiches? I come two thousand miles to work for the fuckers and they have the cheek to give me sandwiches? Oh, fucking hell. Look at the fucking flies.

Mike It's all right. Half of them are dead.

Pete They're not dead, mate. They're kosher. They just hang themselves
upside down

Ami. a kibbutznik in his thirties, appears in the doorway UL. *He carries a pile
of towels. He pauses and listens. He puts the towels down quickly*

Dave Don't you know you're working for fucking Jew boys.

Pete takes a bite of his sandwich and spits it out in the direction of Carrie

Pete Suffering Jesus. This stuff tastes like my granny's armpit.

Carrie crosses R *to get away from Pete*

Ami disappears quickly to make the phone call. Pause

The telephone rings. They all stare at it in silence, wondering what to do

Oh no. Not my fucking mother already.
Dave Not your mother already. Didn't know you spoke Jewish!
Carrie Who's going to answer it?
Pete If it's for me, I'm not in. (*He goes as far away as possible from the tele-
phone and sits in the* DL *chair*)
Carrie It could be for us.

Mike takes a seat at the table

Pete Anyone speak the lingo?

No-one answers

Dave Well, fuck it. Leave it then. Don't want to get tangled up with some cunt
talking fucking gibberish.
Carrie We should answer it. It could be important.
Pete Best of luck.

The telephone continues to ring

Dave Oh, fuck it, I'll do it. (*He crosses to the telephone and lifts the receiver*)
Hello? You speak English? . . . What? . . . Nah, English, you silly pill-
ock . . . What? . . . I don't know what you're talking about. . . . Don't
understand you. Me English. . . . What? . . . From England. England—
hang on. . . . Look . . . just hang on. I'll see if I can find someone. (*He
holds the telephone away from him*) Fuck me, I can't understand a fucking
word. Where'd that geezer with the tommy-gun go?
Pete Don't know.
Dave Shit.

Ami enters and picks up the pile of towels. He stares at Dave

Oh, he'yare. You'll do. Er . . . someone on the telephone. Wants to talk.
To somebody.

Ami remains silent

(*Miming the telephone, pointing to it and using exaggerated gestures*) Somebody ringing. On the telephone. Fucking hell, he doesn't understand me, either.

Ami (*grabbing the telephone; pretending there is somebody talking on the other end*) Ken? Ken? [Yes? Yes?]

Pete We're all right, it's Ken.

Ami (*on the telephone*) Yes, I heard some sporadic shooting.

Dave moves away from the telephone

Dave (*sitting down*) Shit, he can speak fucking English.

Pete Shurrup.

Carrie Quiet!

Mike Quiet!

Ami Yes, it sounded pretty bad. About ten kilometres away. . . . What? It's getting closer? Oh, God. . . . Really? . . . Really? . . . Well, yes, I'll get my rifle. . . . Right. . . . Okay. Shalom. (*He hangs up*)

Dave (*breaking the silence*) You can speak English, then?

Ami hands out towels to them all. Dave, Pete and Carrie rise to their feet

Ami Yes, I speak English.

Carrie Excuse me . . .

Dave (*indicating the towel*) Took you long enough.

Carrie Excuse me . . .

Ami I don't know what you thought you were coming to but this isn't the *Hilton*. If any of you want to share, you'd better pair up now. Someone'll be in shortly to take you to your rooms. Nobody's to move out of here— unless you want a bullet up your arse.

Ami exits

Carrie (*moving to the door*) I say . . . what was all that about shooting?

Pete He said it was getting closer.

Dave Friendly bastard, wasn't he?

Carrie He said he heard shooting.

Dave Be great that, wouldn't it, getting shot on the first fucking day.

Pete Bit scary all that, wasn't it?

Carrie I wonder what's going on?

A silence

Pete Come on, cheer up, you bunch of cunts. I came here to enjoy myself.

Carrie Please! I've got some Valium, should anyone want one. I brought them just in case (*She moves to her haversack*)

Suddenly a deafening, terrifying sound is heard as an aeroplane swoops very low over the roof of the building. Pete dives under the table, Dave falls to the floor, clutching the small towel to his head, and Carrie throws herself among the haversacks. Mike, not in such a panic, picks up his suitcase. The contents spill

Carrie			Oh, God, what is it?
Pete	}	(*together*) {	What's going on? What's going on?
Dave			Mick, Mick, get on the floor!

                                                                        (*etc.*)

Another plane swoops overhead. Mike remains calm and re-packs his suitcase, while the others panic again

> *Gila, a young kibbutznik in her early twenties and dressed in working clothes, enters through the door* UL. *She carries a pair of Wellington boots*

Gila What's this?

They remain cowering

> Why you's on the floor? Someone lose his teeth?

Pete The noise, the noise. What is it? What's going on?

Gila Noise?

An aeroplane swoops again

Gila watches as they cower again

Pete That. That! What is it?

Gila This?

Pete What is it?

Gila They piss on water-melon.

Dave What?

Carrie What's she saying?

Gila I speak English. They piss on water-melon.

Mike They're crop sprayers.

Gila looks at Mike. Pete, Carrie and Dave slowly begin to rise

Pete Crop sprayers? Well, fuck me. (*He goes to the table and sits down*)

Dave I knew it. Fucking hell, I fucking knew it.

Carrie (*sitting down*) Why didn't someone tell us?

Gila (*laughing*) Idiot, you think . . .? (*She puts down her boots and pours some tea*)

Dave Well, what would you think?

Pete Thanks for telling us..Scared seven kinds of shit out of me, that did. Thanks a fucking bunch.

Carrie Do you mind not swearing so much.

Pete Aw, go fuck yourself.

Mike I *was* just about to mention it, actually.

Dave You knew what it was?

Mike I saw it in the fields.

Dave You cunt!

Gila Crazy ass holes. Where you's all coming from?

Pete England.

Gila All you? From England? You's crazy? You think they is coming to bomb your ass into little pieces? (*She takes a sandwich*)

Carrie It sounded so frightening.

Gila Don't worry, the war, she not until August. First we remove water melons for export. We keep you alive till then, at least. After that, who knows? (*She smiles mischievously*)

Carrie What about the gunfire?

Gila What this "gunfire"?

Carrie A kibbutznik. He was talking about gunfire.

Gila Gunfire? If there's being gunfire, tell to me why he's not in bed sucking his thumb and praying for his Mammy?

Dave Well what was it all about, then?

Gila Ask him. (*She puts her tea back on the tea trolley*)

Dave I'll have that bastard. I fucking knew it. He was having us on.

Gila Okay, so I must go work. (*She moves towards the door*) All English? Yuch. My less most favourite person. Take away Shakespeare. He was being good English. But the rest—yuch!

Gila exits UL

Dave Fucking charming.

Mike pours some tea

Pete That's the Jewish manner, mate. Straight to the point, no fucking about. I like it.

Carrie Your language, fellas, honestly.

Pete That's right, darling, *my* language. And don't you forget it.

Dave Hey, Mick, I wouldn't wanna go through all that again, would you?

Mick No. (*He goes and sits at the table*) Thank St Christopher for me again, would you?

Dave Right. Aw get stuffed. I'm sweating cobs.

Gila enters and goes and picks up her boots

Gila Hey, English, which one you's Oswald Mosley? Uh?

Gila laughs and exits with the boots

Dave Who's Oswald Mosley when he's at home?

Pete It's not one of us, is it? Must be some cunt they've been expecting.

Gila enters

Gila Oh, English—welcome to Kibbutz!

Black-out

SCENE 2

The refet (cowshed). Early morning, a week later

The refet has an entrance R *and* L *and is open at the front. There is a strawstack* UR *and a haystack* L, *both of which are covered by tarpaulins with a couple of tyres on top. Two pitchforks lean against the haystack which also has two sets of dungarees draped over it with a pair of working gloves on top. There are two pairs of Wellington boots beside it. Leaning against the strawstack are two shovels, a broom and a pitchfork. Downstage of this, near a tap in the wall* R, *is a large water bin covered by a lid and with a ladle hanging from a handle. There is a toolbox next to the bin and a pile of rope tangled with a hose pipe attached to the tap*

Very bright early morning sunshine streams into the refet and a radio can be heard playing the "Voice of Peace" pop station identity jingle and selections of American hit records

Gila enters UL, *wearing a milking apron and carrying working gloves which she puts on the haystack. She removes three bales of straw from the stack and puts them on the floor, glances at her watch, takes a set of dungarees from the haystack and puts them on the bales of straw. She is about to leave when Mike enters, wearing a sun hat and carrying an orange, cigarettes and matches. A postcard sticks out of his shirt pocket*

Mike Shalom.
Gila You late.
Mike I was told seven-thirty.
Gila Seven-thirty is gone one minute.
Mike So knock a carrot off my wages.
Gila (*pointing*) Work clothes.

Gila exits

Mike picks up the dungarees from the straw bales, removes his hat and begins to change, putting the orange, cigarettes and matches in the dungaree pockets

Mike (*calling*) You couldn't turn that up a bit, could you?

The music stops

Thank you.

Gila enters with a plastic water bottle, goes to the water bin and fills the bottle, and puts it down beside the bin

Lovely day. Gets up in the eighties, I believe. (*After a pause*) Brought my hat. (*He puts it on*) Don't want to dehydrate. It's nice to get into the open air again after a week in the plastics factory.

Gila crosses to the haystack and picks up a pitchfork

Gila Everybody is doing a week there. Don't worry. You're nothing special.

Gila exits with the pitchfork

Mike (*puzzled*) No, I didn't think I was. (*He removes his hat and continue changing*)

Carrie enters

Carrie Good-morning, Michael, and how are you this fine morning?
Mike Wonderful.
Carrie Bags under the eyes, is it?
Mike What?
Carrie Burning the midnight oil.

Mike I don't understand.

Carrie No, I'm not at all surprised, Michael, you're a bit *non compos mentis* this morning. You take your studies seriously, don't you? Thesis, is it?

Mike Sorry?

Carrie Or do they call it a dissertation, I can never quite remember. Don't look so bewildered, Michael. I saw your light on. Last night. Well, really, it was this morning, wasn't it?

Mike Oh, I see.

Carrie Must have been about half-two. I couldn't sleep, you see. The heat. Oh. Atrocious. I'm a Capricorn, you see. Winter's my season. I had to get up in the end and go for a little promenade. That's when I saw your light on. You ought to take it easy, you know; relax a little.

Mike Take what easy?

Mike crosses to the haystack. Carrie follows him

Carrie Studying hard for those exams. Mind you, I do know what it's like when you get into that frame of mind, having had to undergo the rigours of the examination process myself on quite a few occasions. I nurse, you see.

Mike Yes, I know.

Carrie When do you do your finals, then?

Mike Oh, not for another couple of years.

Mike picks up the dungarees from the haystack and hands them to Carrie

Carrie You're doing post-grad, are you?

Mike No.

Carrie So what year are you in.

Mike First.

Carrie But I thought . . . You must have gone up rather late.

Mike Too late.

Carrie You're a mature student, then, are you?

Mike I make no claims.

Carrie How interesting. So what were you doing before you "went up"?

Mike This and that.

Carrie So you haven't been an academic all your life, then?

Mike No.

Carrie So what were you doing before?

Mike Working. Travelling. The usual things.

Carrie starts to put on the dungarees

Carrie Ah, I see. Oh yes. Yes. I must say, I had certain ambitions for higher education myself, but when you receive the call, as they say, those cherished dreams just have to go by the board. Not that I would have attempted to scale the academic heights of an Oxford or a Cambridge, of course, but they do do some very stimulating courses at the Birmingham Polytechnic.

Mike Yes, I can imagine.

Carrie realizes she has dungarees on back to front and changes them

Carrie Mind you, I've taken the precaution of leaving all my nursing manuals at home. If you're going to take a break, it may as well be a clean one.

Carrie finishes changing. Mike climbs the strawstack, as Carrie puts the Wellington boots on

Incidentally, have you been to the kibbutz library yet? Tuesdays seven to nine p.m. They've got some very interesting works. Unfortunately most of them are in Hebrew. But there's quite a stack of paperbacks left behind by other volunteers. It's pretty lightweight, most of it and what isn't lightweight is salacious, so I wouldn't think you'd find much to stimulate you there, but you could try. I was in there last night trying to get some ideas for Volunteers' Day. Not that I managed. You know, of course, we had our second meeting last night. Needless to say, nobody turned up. I sat for half an hour outside the dining-room like a pickle in a jam factory. Oh, don't worry, I'm not getting at you. You were probably busy working, I appreciate that. It's the others I'm worried about.

Mike Which others?

Carrie You know, them. Peter, isn't that his name? And the other one— Dave. A right pair they are, and no mistake. What an advertisement for England.

Gila enters, crosses to haystack and collects a pitchfork

Gila (*to Mike*) You contemplate the universe?
Mike What? (*He gets down*)
Gila So work, come!

Gila thrusts the pitchfork into Mike's hands and exits

Carrie I don't think she likes volunteers. Especially our group.
Mike Really. Why's that?
Carrie Well, didn't you hear them last night? Singing and shouting, waking everybody up. Everyone was talking about it this morning. It was embarrassing walking into the dining-room. They almost smashed the Swedish girls' door down from what I hear.
Mike Who?
Carrie The other two.

Mike smiles

Mike Really?
Carrie Didn't you hear it?
Mike No. But I know they were celebrating.
Carrie Celebrating? Celebrating what, for God's sake?
Mike Why don't you ask them?

Ami enters wheeling a porter's trolley with a water bin on it. He crosses and unloads the bin

Ami Shalom.
Carrie Shalom, Ami. And how are you this fine morning?
Ami Mike . . .

Mike I've got to go. I'll see you later.

Mike exits with the pitchfork

Ami What are you doing here?

Carrie Ah, now, now, Ami. (*Crossing to the empty trolley*) You mean, what am I, a *woman*, doing here? (*She arranges a tyre, a shovel and a broom round the trolley*) I asked if I could "experience" the cowshed for a day. Give me a little break from filling pepper-pots and cleaning up people's slops in the dining-room. Not that I mind. Curious though, isn't it? We used to call that sort of thing "women's work", back in the old, dark days. Still, I like to try my hand at everything, transgress the old demarcations as it were, and, of course, the marvellous thing about the cowshed here is that there are so many ideal spots for a bit of sketching. I paint, you see. (*She points to her "arrangement"*)

Ami Yes, I've noticed.

Carrie I mean, the "official tour", as it were, good though it was, was a little cursory. It's the nooks and crannies, isn't it, not the highways and byeways, that are interesting? Especially when you've got a painter's eye. (*Pause*) So—what shall we do then?

Ami Watch, I show you.

Ami crosses to the haystack and Carrie follows him

This hay. Hazir in Hebrew. (*He lifts the tarpaulin so she can see*)

Carrie Hazir.

Ami This is what the cows eat. Okay?

Carrie They eat hazir.

Ami moves to the strawstack. Carrie follows

Ami This—straw. Cache. This is what the cows walk on. Understand?

Carrie Hay they eat, straw they walk on.

Ami Hazir, this you don't touch, okay? But the cache—cache is blonde, okay, like pretty girl, remember this way—you'll find bales of this stacked above the cow pens. Reach up and throw a couple in—(*Ami throws a straw bale to the ground*)—two between every post. Then you must go into the cowshit, cut off the string. (*Ami takes a knife from his pocket and cuts the string off*) Kick it all over the dung . . .

Ami kicks the bale around. Carrie helps

And keep all the bits of string. Okay? Bring them to me.

Carrie I think I can manage.

Ami hands her the string from the open bale

Ami And any you see, bring them also. They have to be fished out of the shit, otherwise the cows get their legs tangled.

Carrie I don't mind a bit of dirty work.

Ami moves to the trolley and dismantles the "arrangement"

Ami Good. So why you wait?

Carrie I was just admiring your command of the English tongue, Ami.
Ami This we can do some other time. Now we must work.
Carrie Right. Right.

Carrie exits

Ami starts to go out with the trolley

Gila and Mike enter with a wheelbarrow

Ami (*seeing Gila and Mike and stopping*) Gila, we must bring some hay from the fields. Where is the tractor?
Gila I fetch it.
Ami Just tell me where it is.
Gila I fetch it.

Ami raises his arms and exits with the trolley

Mike watches as Gila collects the gloves from the haystack and shovels from against the strawstack and puts them into the wheelbarrow

Mike Is it me or does humanity in general disgust you?
Gila Uh?
Mike I must say, it's stimulating working with you.

Gila throws the tyres from the haystack and pushes the tarpaulin off

Gila Uh? Stim-u-lating? What this?
Mike Interesting. Exciting. The clashing of minds, the interchange of ideas, the discovery of the cultural reference points. All the things we've been discussing.
Gila What?
Mike Just what I came for.

Gila gets three bales of hay down

Gila (*loading the hay on to the barrow*) Uh?
Mike Uh? Is that all you can manage?
Gila Uh?
Mike Uh? Uh? You ought to put music to it. Probably do very well in the Eurovision Song Contest.
Gila What you talk about?
Mike Talk? I've been here an hour, I've heard no talk.
Gila Ah . . . (*She picks up the plastic water bottle from beside the water bins*) What you do on kibbutz?
Mike I meant to get off the plane at Stockholm, it's all a big mistake.
Gila Uh?
Mike Uh?
Gila How long you plan stay on kibbutz?
Mike About another half-hour.
Gila You have much problem back in England?
Mike No. Why?
Gila So why you volunteer? (*She puts the bottle in the barrow*)

Mike Do you mind if I stop a minute? I'm not used to working in this kind of heat.

Gila What are you, little child must always keep ask his Mummy? You want to stop, so stop.

Mike takes the plastic bottle from the barrow

Mike You don't like volunteers, I hear?

Gila Ah, pain in the ass.

Mike drinks in large gulps

You try for being last passenger on *Titanic*?

Mike Sorry could you say that again in English?

Mike drinks again

Gila This.

Mike We've been instructed to drink ten pints a day, at least. Otherwise we collapse.

Gila You have to drink in one sit?

Mike Sorry? I didn't quite understand a word of that.

Gila We have many works to do. (*She turns away*) Shit, all volunteers stupid idiot.

Mike (*turning away*) And all Jews have long noses.

Gila (*turning back quickly*) What you say?

Mike Sorry, I was speaking English, you wouldn't understand.

Gila takes a handful of hay and thrusts it under Mike's nose

Gila This. Food for cow. They very much liking to eat, you understand? All night they's talking to each other about this: "We wait for morning, we eat." Come, work!

Mike In England we have a custom. We say please and thank you.

Gila Cow can't say please. Cow can't say thank you.

Mike No, but if you and I are going to go on working together, you're going to have to get into the habit.

Gila Bullshit.

Mike No — manners.

Gila Drink, drink. Drown!

Mike throws the bottle in the barrow and takes his cigarettes from his pocket. He gets one out of the packet

What this?

Mike We call them cig-a-rettes.

Gila Bloody hell. You here to work. (*She grabs the cigarette and stamps it out*)

Mike I'm here to make holiday.

Gila First you work, then make holiday!

Mike I'm afraid there's been some misunderstanding. Your priorities are not mine. Shall we start again? My name's Mike. (*He offers his hand*)

Gila So?

Mike Fair enough. (*He sits on straw bales*) It does say semi-arid desert on the map.

Gila sits herself on a bale of hay in the barrow and stares very intently into the distance

Sorry to bother you, but what are you doing?

Gila We check for hornies.

Mike Ah, yes. (*Pause*) Would it be too much trouble to tell me what hornies is?

Gila You want to know?

Mike Why not?

Gila Huh. In all the time I work in refet, never once does volunteer ask me this question.

Mike You *can* form sentences.

Gila You want to know? Serious?

Mike Sure.

Gila Shit, I don't believe. Okay, so cow, if she is not pregnant, is feeling like she want to be screwed every twenty-one days.

Mike My wife was exactly the same.

Gila You married?

Mike Joke?

Gila Uh?

Mike Sick joke. Doesn't matter. You were saying?

Gila You *really* want to know this?

Mike Yes.

Gila (*very quickly; deliberately trying to confuse*) Okay, so cow want to be screwed every twenty-one days, so we is looking for the hornies. Hornie is the bull, separate to jump on her to screw. But she is running after other and want him to jump on her. Usual, we tell this by her having red pussy. So we must pull out to insimilate her because otherwise cow is give birth. Then, when she is having had birth, after forty day we let her bosom rest, dry her and get her back pregnant 'cos she is to have birth again, full of milk.

Gila looks at Mike

Mike Ah yes.

Gila Okay? (*Pause*) What you look at? There's something wrong with me?

Mike No, no. Far from it.

Gila My English, she's good?

Mike Different.

Gila This good?

Mike Can be.

Gila You understand?

Mike The first sentence—magic.

Gila Ah, you learn. Come. (*She gets up from the hay bale*) We take out number two-four-zero. He want to screw.

Mike (*looking at her*) Yes, I can quite believe it.

Carrie enters carrying a large bundle of shitty string. Her face is dirty

Carrie Shalom, Gila. And how are you this fine morning?

Gila and Mike exit with the barrow-load of hay. Ami enters carrying a large wooden palette and crosses to the haystack. He puts the palette on the ground

I've collected all the string.

Ami Good. Good.

Carrie What shall I do with it?

Ami I'll put it in the incinerator. (*He untangles the rope from the hosepipe, and disconnects the hose from the tap*)

Carrie Can I ask a question? About Volunteers' Day? Of course, I realize it's your responsibility ultimately as Volunteers' Liaison Officer, so please don't be afraid to say if I'm stepping on toes, but I was wondering if I might make a little suggestion?

Ami Go ahead.

Carrie Well, the exercise seems to be to put on a show for kibbutzniks, to give some idea of our lives back home. Some aspect of our culture. I have understood correctly?

Ami Yes. (*He starts coiling the rope*)

Carrie Well, how about some poetry, perhaps? That would be rather nice, don't you think?

Ami It's perhaps a little early to start making decisions.

Carrie Well, our group is not exactly what one would call eager, Ami. There was a meeting last night. Nobody turned up. I've called another at lunch-time. I think in the end we may have to impose.

Ami Who is we?

Carrie Well, you and I, Ami. Nobody else seems interested.

Ami Don't worry, I have it arranged.

Carrie I suppose I have taken upon myself the awesome task of being "group leader" as nobody else——

Ami Let's talk about it some other time. It's not for a long time yet. (*He hangs the rope on the hook* DR *and coils the hose*)

Carrie Yes, I know, but our group, Ami. They're not much of an advertise-ment, are they? Talk about cultural poverty. Not that the other groups are much different. I get the impression that most of the girls are here for one reason and one reason only, and that has nothing to do with studying socialism. I don't think I would have come if I'd known it was going to be like this.

Ami What *are* you doing here?

Carrie What am *I* doing here? I came for a holiday. Obviously.

Ami So how long you plan to stay.

Carrie It all rather depends upon my chap, really. He's a doctor, you see. He's . . . been called to Africa. They've created a post specially for him and . . . obviously I couldn't go along too, so I'm . . . filling in time. More or less.

Ami It's true you're a nurse in England?

Carrie What do you mean is it true? Yes, I'm a nurse; lots of people are nurses, what's so strange about that, why shouldn't I be one?

Ami Did I say you're not?

Carrie Well it's just the way you said that. I mean . . .

Mike enters with wheelbarrow which now contains three bags of concrete mix.
He proceeds to unload the bags on to the palette

Carrie (*picking up the string*) I'll go and put this in the incinerator shall I?
Ami I'll do it.
Carrie I don't mind doing it, Ami. I'm not completely incapable.
Ami Okay, so if you want so do it. And when you've done that help Gila and
  Mike feed the cows. But first—take a break, relax a little.
Carrie I'll take my break when everybody else takes theirs, thank you very
  much.

Carrie exits abruptly with her string

Ami Shit, what did I say? Hamitnadvim hae'lu yeshagu otanu legamrei!
  [These volunteers will drive us all crazy too!]
Mike Hey, Ami—Gila, she's not a member, is she?
Ami Gila? No.
Mike Her parents don't live on the kibbutz?
Ami They're living in Tel Aviv.
Mike So what's she doing here?
Ami She belongs to an army unit. They have the choice of doing their last
  year of military service on kibbutz. It's a way of encouraging new settlers.
Mike Really? Interesting.
Ami I can lend you some books, if you want to read more.
Mike So she's not a daughter of the kibbutz?
Ami No, I don't think you'll find what you want in a book. Listen, I must
  have words with you.

Gila enters

(*Seeing Gila*) We'll talk later.

Ami picks up the hosepipe and exits with it

Mike sits on the bags of concrete mix

Gila What you do here?
Mike Tea break.
Gila Tea break?
Mike (*looking at his watch*) Ten o'clock.
Gila Come, work.
Mike No can do, I'm afraid. Official.
Gila What? What this?
Mike Tea break, mate.

Mike takes the orange from his pocket and begins to peel it

Gila Shit, I don't believe my ear.
Mike Where?
Gila What is this?
Mike English custom, Charlie. Ten minutes rest. Sandwiches, complaints
  about the wife, Social Security scroungers, tax fiddlers . . .

Gila Uh?

Mike And jokes. You tell me a joke, I tell you a joke. Preferably something sexual but if you can't manage that, something about the wife.

Gila What?

Mike So come on, tell me a joke. Entertain me.

Gila, amazed, flops down heavily on the nearest available surface

Not bad, not bad. Bit physical. No that's probably very funny to you lot, probably goes down a wow that one, but we go in for a bit more of the verbal. Try again.

Gila I don't know what the fuck you talk about.

Mike In England, we have this tradition. Break time is a time for silliness, sexual ambiguity. It's a working-class habit. Some slight respite from tedium. Are you still awake?

Gila You Jewish?

Mike No, you? (*Pause*) Wanna hear a nice Jewish joke?

Gila stares at him

Oh, well.

Pause

Gila Give joke.

Mike I've rather gone off the idea. All right, here we go. (*He rises to his feet*) You'll like this. It's about one of your mob. Stalin——

Gila Stalin? He one of ours? You crazy?

Mike Hold on, hold on, I haven't even started yet. Stalin was addressing the Third Congress. "I have here," he said, "a most historic document. A telegram of congratulations from Leon Trotsky." He reads the telegram. "Joseph Stalin, The Kremlin, Moscow. You were right and I was wrong. You are the true heir of Lenin. I should apologize. Trotsky."

Gila You think this is funny? (*Slapping her forehead*) Oy, yoy, yoy.

Mike You think this is the end of the joke? (*Imitating her slap*) Oy, yoy, yoy. So Stalin reads the telegram and there's a roar of approval from the crowd. But in the front row, there's a little Jewish tailor——

Gila You anti-semitic?

Mike If you keep interrupting there's no telling what may happen. Can I go on?

Gila gestures "if you like"

The little Jewish tailor goes, "Psst! Psst, Comrade Stalin!" Stalin leans over to hear what he has to say. "Such a message," says the little tailor. "Such a message. But you read it without the right feeling." "What!" says Stalin, amazed. "If you think you can do better get up here." So the little tailor jumps on to the podium and says to Stalin, "You've got to remember Trotsky was a Jew. This is how it should be read." And he reads it out. "You were *right* and I was *wrong*? *You* are the true heir of Lenin? *I* should apologize?" (*He begins to laugh*) No? Oh, well.

Gila (*getting up*) English person, keep work. Do the stack.

Mike And where are you going?

Gila I must make shit.

Mike Again? You made shit half an hour ago.

Gila So I make more.

Mike I make shit, too, you know. I'd dearly love to make it. There's nothing
I'd enjoy more. I've been wanting to make shit all morning. Aching for it.

Gila You want, so make it.

Mike I don't get time to make it. Someone's got to work around here. You've
got this shitting business wrapped up.

Gila Young English person . . .

Mike And how come, while we're on about work, how come while I'm stack-
ing haystacks, you're driving the tractor? While I'm breaking my back un-
loading hay, you're driving the tractor? While I'm wading through cowshit,
cleaning out, you're driving the tractor? In fact, when there's the remotest
possibility of you ever having to do any *real* work, you're driving the
tractor — or making shit?

Gila Volunteer not allowed to ride tractor, you know this.

Mike Right. Too fucking right. Because you keep all the decent jobs for your
fucking selves!

Gila You — work!

Mike Look, I'm here to help you, right? Help. I've no intention of doing all
the work myself. Okay? I'm doing this for nothing remember. You're not
even paying me. I'm here because I want to be. And if I don't like it, I can
turn around and walk away. Okay? So just remember that!

Gila English person — I remember this since I was so high. Come, work.

*Gila stares at Mike who doesn't move. She turns away and appears to be crying.
Mike is angry that he has upset her and turns away. Pause. It is now apparent
that Gila is, in fact, laughing*

(*Turning back to Mike*) Ha, ha, ha. I like this. "*You* were right *and* I was
wrong. You *are* the true heir of Lenin. I *should* apologize." Hey, I like this.
This is good joke.

Mike Well, that's one way of looking at it.

Gila Okay, so . . . what your name — Mike?

Mike nods

Okay, so no more shit.

Mike Promise?

Gila Promise. You want to ride tractor?

Mike I thought . . .

Gila Ah, bullshit. I make the rule as I go along. Come, we must work. "*You*
were right and I *was* wrong. You *are* the true heir of Lenin. I should *apologize*." Shit this good joke . . .

Gila exits

Mike moves to follow her

Ami enters with a coil of wire

Ami Hey, Mike, can you give me a moment?

Mike I should be working.

Ami Ah, just a minute, no more. I have to organize this now or we never get done. (*He starts searching in the toolbox for staples*)

Mike Organize what?

Ami I call round to your house to see you last night. Your light is on but you weren't there.

Mike No, I was out, celebrating.

Ami Yes, I've heard about it.

Mike Sorry, we did get a little drunk.

Ami This is your business. What I want to say to you is we need somebody from your group to act as group leader and to organize your contribution to Volunteers' Day.

Mike Oh, I'm afraid . . . No thanks.

Ami Mike, I don't understand you. We talk a few nights. I think we are friends.

Mike nods

So why, when we are talking about Volunteers' Day, you are treating me like I have leprosy?

Mike I'm sorry, I just . . .

Ami I want to know why does nobody turn up for the meetings?

Mike Apathy.

Ami But why?

Mike We're English, Ami, what do you expect?

Ami Carrie tells me you can't agree on what's typically English.

Mike That's typically English.

Ami This is not a joke, Mike.

Mike No. Sorry.

Ami You know, we are a small, enclosed society. One hundred-twenty families. We need volunteers. We need them so that we are not becoming small, enclosed people. But it's important they fit in. Otherwise there's no point. For them, for us. Mike, I'm not going to treat you like a child, but please—don't say any of this to the others in your group. Volunteers' Day. Okay. It's to be taken seriously. You must put on a show. But . . . every year for twenty years the Australians give us *Waltzing Matilda*; the Swiss a drinking song. So no great surprises. We don't expect miracles. The real point of the exercise is that if you are going to live our way of life, you must experience what it is like for us. The problems that confront us; how we resolve them. And so on. So you must think of your group, not as individuals, but as a small community. You understand?

Mike Yes. Perfectly.

Ami Good. The point is, Mike, it isn't easy but this is our way and you also must try. For most of you it will be a new experience but one which, we hope, will be worthwhile. However, I think that with your group I may need some help. So what do you say? You'll be group leader?

Mike No.

Ami Mike——

Mike I'm sorry, I really don't want to.
Ami Why?
Mike I'd just prefer not to.
Ami Why not, it won't take up much of your time?
Mike I'd really rather not.
Ami But why?
Mike Oh . . . lots of reasons.
Ami Such as?
Mike Ask Carrie. She'll do it.
Ami She is not the best person.
Mike I'm sorry. I really should be working.

Mike starts to go but Ami delays him

Ami You know, Mike, I work here in the refet now for almost a year. Last year I was secretary of the kibbutz. Next year I am back in the gardens. Which job you think I like best?
Mike Don't know.
Ami The gardens. I am alone. The flowers don't shout back. Everybody loves me. I have no responsibilities.
Mike I should be working.

Mike exits. Ami stares after him, then exits with the wire and toolbox

Quick fade

Dave, carrying a large plastic bucket, and Gila, carrying a bag of concrete mix, enter in the darkness. Dave lies down behind the front bales of hay so that he is hidden from view

When the Lights come up again it is late afternoon and the working pace is much slower than before. Gila is adding a bag of concrete mix to the pile on the palette

Mike enters carrying another bag

Mike That's it.
Gila Uh?
Mike No more. Finished. (*He sits on one of the bags*) What's it all for?
Gila Uh?
Mike All this concrete. What's it for?
Gila (*sitting beside him*) In Israel, we is having law which is saying . . . "no pig can be kept on the land", because this land, she is . . . er . . . there is a word . . . from the Bible . . . you know, because this land is . . . holy land . . . you understand?
Mike Sacred?
Gila Ken, ken. [Yes, yes.] "Sacred" land. So, if no pig must ever touch the land because it is sacred . . . okay—it live on concrete. There's being nothing in the Bible about concrete. Smart, huh?

They both laugh

Carrie enters slowly, wheeling the trolley. She looks exhausted. She stops by the three straw bales and flops down on them

Carrie Gosh, I'm shattered. This heat.

Gila (*getting to her feet*) You make closer the food?

Carrie Sorry, Gila?

Gila You make football with the cow food?

Carrie No. I thought you'd——

Gila So do this, then we can go home, okay? Mike, I check your work. If everything's good, we finish.

Mike What shall I do?

Gila Ah, rest your ass.

Gila exits

Carrie gets up wearily and goes to the haystack

Carrie I think I'll be glad to get back to the dining-room . . . (*She takes a hay bale and puts it on the floor*) I feel like I've done a fortnight's work already. It never seems to finish. And now, more.

She takes a second bale and puts it on the floor, not seeing that Dave is now revealed sleeping in the haystack

Mike I'll do it if you like.

Carrie I can manage.

Carrie turns to collect a third bale, sees Dave and screams. Dave wakes and sits up abruptly. Mike laughs

Mike I thought you were working in the factory?

Dave grabs the large plastic bucket and rag and staggers off with them

Dave (*as he goes*) Water. Water!

Pete (*off*) Hey bollocks.

Mike (*shouting*) What?

Pete (*off*) You got any fags?

Mike (*calling*) I'd give you one but I've only got nineteen left.

Carrie puts the bales on the trolley

Carrie You know, I think there must be a special office in Tel Aviv where they get them all from.

Mike Who?

Carrie Those idiots. Best thing, I find, is to keep away from them. Ignore them completely. Don't sully yourself.

Mike Christ, I envy you your certainty.

Carrie (*smiling*) About what?

Mike Everything. To be certain about anything must be nice.

Carrie Sorry, I don't quite understand . . .

Pete cycles in, throws the bike against the strawstack and makes a mock attack on Mike for a cigarette

Pete Come on, cunt, give us one.

Carrie Proud of yourself, are you? You're not in the gutter now, you know.
Pete (*dangerously*) What?

Carrie screams and exits quickly, leaving the trolley

Mike (*restraining him*) Forget it.
Pete Cheeky bitch, who's she think she is? Comes up to me lunchtime, says; "There's a meeting tonight about the English group's contribution to Volunteers' Day. Eight-fifteen. Be there." Not so much as a please or thank you. Told her to go fuck herself. (*Shouting after her*) Jumped up shithouse!
Mike Here. (*He takes the cigarettes from his pocket*)
Pete Ain't right, though, is it, being spoken to like that?
Mike Only Umaya I'm afraid.
Pete Aw, you get cancer just looking at those. I'd swing for a Woodbine. (*He takes a cigarette and puts it in his pocket*)
Mike How's life over in the chicken sheds?
Pete What? Ah, someone must have told them, I reckon. (*He sits beside Mike*)
Mike What?
Pete That I grew up on a poultry farm. Funny isn't it? I grew up with the fuckers and here I am working with them again. I've been in and out of chickens all my fucking life.
Mike Dirty bleeder.
Pete What? (*He laughs*) Nah, serious.
Mike Ask for a transfer.
Pete Nah, no way, man. Chickens are funny things. They've got minds of their own. They need a professional looking after them. They can tell when there's an amateur about. No, they *need* me there. They need my expertise.
Mike How's your head?
Pete (*getting up*) Aw, don't remind me. Shit, was I pissed last night. Ooh, fuck me. (*He takes a pitchfork from the strawstack and prods a bale of hay*) What happened to you, then? What time did you get home?
Mike Some time.
Pete Last I saw of you, you was trying to persuade that fat Australian tart, Grace, to go for a swim — with her clothes off, you kinky bastard. Pull her did you? Eh?
Mike I can't remember. She wasn't there in the morning.
Pete You should have stayed with us. We was a bit naughty, I think, me and Dave. Burst in on the Swedish tarts after you disappeared. Ugh! No-go area. Mind you, it was half-two in the morning. They speak the Old Inglaisie well. Told us to fuck off. Yeh, straight up. "Get out and fuck off, please." We wanted to put the light on, you know, have a bit of a dance. Mind you, have you seen the two Finnish tarts? They're even worse. If they smile in the next month, I'll eat your arse.

Mike laughs

They don't, you know.
Mike What?

Pete Smile. Against their religion or something. Land of the midnight sun and all that. Makes them fucking miserable for some reason. Mind you, now that I've got an extra couple of hundred quid being sent out, I'll be buying it more than likely. Tel Aviv, Jerusalem. Sample the delights. Got a whole fucking box of Durex, didn't I, to bring out here with me? Left them behind as well. I was gonna get the old girl to fish 'em out from behind the wardrobe but I thought, you know, bit fucking tactless. Especially as her and the old man haven't been seeing eye-to-eye in that department for, you know, a good fifteen or twenty years.

Mike Did you get through all right?

Pete Clean as a bell. With a satellite, even your fucking mother's just around the corner. (*He tosses the pitchfork into the strawstack*)

Mike Everything okay?

Pete Was till I spoke to the old man. I said I'm out here for three months. He said how much are they paying you? I said would you believe, I'm working with the chickens again? He said how much are they paying you? I said some days I have to get up at four in the morning and start work without any breakfast. He said how much are they paying you? I said I'm working an eight-hour day and wasting away 'cos all we get to eat are raw vegetables. He said how much are they paying you? I said I'm so knackered at the end of the day, I just sleep all evening. He said how much are they paying you? I said nothing. He said what? I said nothing. They're burying him on Monday. (*He crosses to the water bin, drinks and puts the ladle on the back of his head*) His last words were: "Come home, Hymie. If *that's* the Promised Land, come home." (*He gets a broom from the haystack and begins to sweep up the loose straw*)

Mike You're not Jewish are you?

Pete Jewish? If I was Jewish, do you think I'd be stupid enough to work under these conditions? Eh? Now I understand why a Jewish volunteer is about as common as a pork chop at a Bar Mitzvah. (*He throws the broom down and then sits in the space he's cleared*) They've got more fucking sense. (*He sniffs the air*) Mind you, that ain't everything, is it? (*He sniffs again*) Shit, you ought to take a shower now and again you know.

Mike It's the boots.

Pete Come off it, you smelt like that the day we arrived.

Gila enters and goes to Mike

Gila Young English person, what farm you grow up on — funny farm?

Mike What's the matter?

Gila For twenty years we give the cow hay to eat and straw to stand on. We hear no complaint from them. You know how much this hay cost?

Mike What have I done?

Gila Now you's come to kibbutz and they's walk on hay like they's staying at the *King David Hotel*, and, poor bastards, they's try to eat straw like they was Yemenis.

Mike Cache means straw? Ugh. I thought it was the other way around.

Gila Idiot. This waste hundred of dollar.

Mike Well, if you will insist on speaking this Biblical slang.

Gila What?

Mike I'm sorry.

Gila Sorry? Sorry won't give us milk. Sorry won't not put no money in the bank.

Gila exits

Pete Aye-aye, aye-aye, what's all this about you growing up on a farm, then?

Mike If you want to work here permanently, you have to have some experience.

Pete What do you want to work here permanently for? Keep away from the rest of us?

Mike No. (*He smiles*)

Pete Oh, I get you. You crafty bastard. Ooh, *I* don't half fancy a bit of crumpet, an' all.

Mike There's always the Australian girl.

Pete Grace? Ugh, fuck that.

Mike You may have to.

Pete Ugh, no way, man.

Gila enters

Gila Mike, why you spread cache like this? (*She mimes spreading it ever-so-evenly*)

Mike I thought you wanted it evenly spread.

Gila Don't worry so careful. The cows have never heard of socialism!

Gila exits

Pete (*picking up the bike*) I'd better go strangle some chickens. See you at supper.

Mike Save a table.

Pete Right. You know there's another meeting about this Volunteers' Day business. You got any ideas?

Mike Ignore it.

Pete Oh. Right. Good one. Come round and play some tapes before supper. If you're not "too busy". (*He cycles in a circle and winks*) Shalom.

Mike Shalom.

Pete Means "peace", that, you know. The Arabs say "salem". I was reading up on it.

Gila enters

Pete stands astride his bike

Gila Mike!

Mike Oh, what now?

Gila I find your bootmark all over the cows' food. Why you walk on the cows' food?

Mike It's only hay.

Gila Uh? Only hay? You walk on your own food?

Mike No.

Gila So tell to me—why the cows so different from you?

Mike I don't eat anything standing in three feet of shit.

Pete laughs hugely

Gila (*shaking her head*) Crazy ass-hole. I see if you do anything right this day.

    Gila exits

Pete See you later. Oi, Golda!

    Pete, still laughing, exits on his bike

Mike begins to change out of his working gear

    Carrie enters, crosses to the water bin and takes a long drink, then goes and sits on a bale of hay

Mike (*sitting beside her*) You know, if we're going to get this Volunteers' Day show off the ground, we're going to have to start working as a group.

Carrie I know. It's going to be very difficult.

Mike And, first of all, you're going to have to learn a few things about how to treat people.

Carrie Me treat people?

Mike Yes.

Carrie Oh, I see. You mean, like that idiot?

Mike What makes you so certain?

Carrie He's only got to open his mouth. I mean, that's the problem with our group, isn't it? There are two distinct sides. There's you and me—and there's them. Quite honestly, I think the best thing would be for us to do something separately. Then they can get up there and make a holy show of themselves. Where do they get them from, that's what I'd like to know?

Mike Exactly the same place they got you from.

Carrie What do you mean?

Mike I mean that they get them from exactly the same fucking place they got you from.

Carrie Oh, really? How would you know.

Mike You've only got to open your mouth.

She gets up, moves away and sits on the strawstack

    Gila enters

Gila (*to Mike*) So, young English person—*finito la commedia*. Many, many mistake, but you learn. So what the problem?

Mike (*pointing to the sun*) You couldn't get Him to turn that down a bit, could you? I believe you lot have some sort of special relationship.

Gila laughs and slaps Mike on the back

Gila So, Mister Mike, thank you mostest kindly please for work which you doing today and sincerely please and this is coming from the bottom of my heart, terribly, terribly thank you. (*She sits beside him*) Shit, I'm absolutely tired. Today, she's good day, isn't it? I don't have such good day for so long time. (*She slaps Mike on the back again*)

Mike No wonder. I did all the work. (*He slaps Gila on the back in return*)
Gila Sure. This is what you here for.

She slaps him again and he gives up

Hey, Mike, you ride horse in Cambridge?
Mike Only in the rush-hour.
Gila You want I should teach you?
Mike Yes, great. Today?
Gila Sure. But first we shower and then eat a little. I'm absolutely hungry. My
stomach begins to make poetry. (*She rubs her stomach*)
Mike I'll do that if you like.
Gila Uh?
Mike Doesn't matter.

Pause

Gila Hey, Mike, tell to me. What you do in kibbutz?
Mike I do all the work in the cowshed, what do you do?

Gila laughs. She notices Mike's postcard in his shirt pocket

Gila (*pointing to it*) What this?
Mike It's a postcard — to my parents.
Gila Read it to me.
Mike (*taking it from his pocket and reading*) "Dear Mum and Dad. Got here
safe and sound. Weather marvellous. Food tolerable. Bit like Butlin's, only
run on socialist lines. Dad'll explain what socialism means." Don't know
why I bother. They won't know what the hell I'm talking about, anyway.
How best would you describe the kibbutz? "Socialism with reservations"
or "reservations with socialism"?
Gila Depends why you want to say it. You tell them why you leave uni-
versity?
Mike I don't know why.
Gila So how you think to tell them?
Mike If I stay here long enough, maybe something will occur to me.
Gila I'm thinking not.
Mike No, maybe not.
Gila You know, one of the unique things about kibbutz life is you have to be
elected; to go before the Selection Committee and give why you want to
belong, what you're able to offer the community.
Mike Yes.
Gila Each people have made a conscience commitment . . .
Mike Conscious commitment.
Gila Okay. Conscious commitment, to way of life, also to ideology. So
kibbutz is ideological collective. This is why it works. You see?
Mike I'm not sure.
Gila Well, point being is you can't . . . drift, know what I mean? Into kibbutz life. Volunteering is the same. There is no place here for drifters. You
have to be involved. You have to know why you're here, why you come,
what you looking for.

Mike How do you find that out?
Gila I think you must know before you come. And I don't think you know.
I don't think you know why you are on kibbutz.

Ami enters

Ami Gila, haim he'evart et hakavim? [Gila, have you done the pipes?]
Gila Ken. [Yes.]
Ami Ken? [Yes?]
Gila Ken. [Yes.]
Ami Natat ochel la parot? [Did you feed the cows?]
Gila Ken. [Yes.]
Ami Ken? [Yes?]
Gila Ken, ken. [Yes, yes.]
Ami Keravt et haochel? [Did you push the cowfood closer?]
Gila Ken. [Yes.]
Ami So—roza hafsaka? [So—you want a break?]
Gila (*smiling*) Ken. [Yes.]
Ami (*quietly*) Roza lenashek le et hatachat? [You want to kiss my ass?]

Gila laughs and takes a swipe at him

Ami runs off

Mike What was all that about?
Gila He wants to know first of all, if we's doing all the work and second, if I
want to kiss his ass.
Mike Ah. A charming man.

Gila turns to Carrie

Gila Carrie, thank you very much for your work—and goodbye.
Carrie Shalom.

Carrie exits

Gila Listen, young English person. I speak English, you know, not highly,
but I know there is being something which you don't say. I mean, as far as
I'm going, I'm not philosopher, but I'm give you, if this what you want, to
listen. I'm not a fool, you know. So . . .?

Ami rushes on holding his shirt over a deep cut in his hand

Ami Shit! Carrie!
Mike What have you done?
Ami Shout this girl for me! She's a nurse, yes?
Mike (*shouting off to Carrie*) Carrie! Quickly!
Gila Ami, eich asita et ze? [Ah, Ami, how did you do this?]
Ami This is my writing hand. Shit! Shit! It's painful!
Mike Do you have a first-aid box?
Gila Yes, I get.

Gila runs off

Mike Sit down.

He helps Ami across to the straw bales

What happened?
Ami The bloody tractor blade. Ah . . .
Mike I'm sorry, I don't know what to do.
Ami Damn, it's painful.
Mike It looks deep.

Carrie rushes in and across to them

Carrie What's the matter, what's going on?
Ami I cut my hand. I need some help.

Ami holds his hand out to show her. Carrie faints

What the bloody hell . . .?

Gila enters, carrying a first-aid box, and sees Carrie

Gila Uh?
Ami I thought this girl said she is nurse.
Mike That's what she said.
Gila Shit. So much for your National Health Service.

Black-out

ACT II

Scene 1

The kibbutz swimming-pool. Summer, late afternoon, a month later

The top section of the swimming-pool ladder is fixed to the front edge of the stage, indicating that the pool forms the "fourth wall". There are two palm trees upstage and behind them a large fence stretching across the rear wall, with a gate in the middle. DR *there is a shower hut and* DL *a fixed rail holding two towels. Near the rail is a sunbed and* C *is a garden table with an umbrella and two chairs. Another two chairs and table (without an umbrella) stands* DR *near the shower hut*

As the Lights come up Mike is seated at the table DR, *wearing swimming-shorts and with a towel thrown over the back of the chair. He is trying to write a letter but is constantly interrupted by Carrie who is lying on her towel on the sunbed, wearing a swimsuit and sun hat. Like all the English group, the two of them have a deep suntan by now*

Mike slams his pen down

Mike Damn. (*He picks up his pen again*)
Carrie Isn't this peaceful?
Mike Yes.

Each time Mike tries to make a fresh start, Carrie speaks. His irritation grows

Carrie Isn't it lovely?
Mike Yes.

Slight pause. He starts again

Carrie I could stay here forever. (*Pause*) I'm not sure if I can sit here much longer, though. (*Pause*) I like to be active. Do you know what I mean?
Mike Yes.
Carrie I should be painting. (*Pause*) I like to keep busy. (*Pause*) Am I disturbing you?
Mike No.
Carrie What are you doing?
Mike Trying to write a letter.
Carrie You've been doing that all afternoon.
Mike Yes.
Carrie Is it the same one?
Mike Yes, it's the same one.
Carrie Everything takes so long in this heat, doesn't it? I've been lying here

for . . . oh, it must be at least two hours—trying to summon up the energy just to get up . . . I just can't seem to. (*Pause*) How long are you planning to stay?

Mike Mmm?

Carrie How long are you planning to stay on the kibbutz?

Mike Erm . . . I don't know. I haven't thought about it.

Carrie I don't know what I'll do when I leave here. I'm really enjoying myself. I don't think I've been as happy as this in . . . oh, a long while.

Mike What about your boyfriend, don't you miss him?

Carrie Yes, yes. Of course I do. But I've my own life to lead. (*She gets to her feet and folds up the sunbed, suddenly*) I can't sit here all day. I think I'll do some painting. I started on the trees over there. It's coming on quite nicely. Bye, Michael.

Carrie exits, carrying the sun bed, very quickly

Mike (*looking puzzled*) Bye, Carrie. (*He goes on writing*)

After a moment Gila enters wearing a swimming costume, and with a towel around her shoulders. Her manner to Mike is very stiff and formal

Gila Shalom.

Mike Hello. How are you?

Gila Fine. And how are you today?

Mike Fine thanks. And you?

Gila Very well, thank you.

Mike Good. Good.

Gila smiles stiffly. Pause

Gila You mind if I sit down?

Mike Of course not. Please . . . (*He indicates the chair beside him*)

Gila sits down carefully, making a great play of doing it properly

Gila The weather is beautiful, isn't she?

Mike Very pleasant.

Gila What is this?

Mike I'm trying to write a letter.

Gila To your lover in England?

Mike To my parents.

Gila How it's going?

Mike Not very well, I'm afraid.

Gila To write to one's parents is difficult, I'm thinking.

Mike Yes, it is.

Gila I write to my Mamma sometimes, but to my Pappa, never. (*Pause*) My father is being Gulliver as far as his mind is concern but Lilliput in so far as we speak of his lifestyle.

Mike looks puzzled

He drink too much.

Gila I'm making clarify?
Mike Yes, very clarify.

Gila smiles hugely

Gila I've just been talking with some of your friends outside the dining-room. I guess kibbutz is shelter for a lot of crazies. A lot of crazies come to kibbutz. You get food and a bed. I tell them, why come here? You can do kibbutz in London in youth hostel.
Mike You certainly know how to endear yourself to people.
Gila Sure, I guess this is why they don't like my guts.
Mike No, no, no, no, no. Not "don't like my guts".
Gila Why not?
Mike You've got it all mixed up again. English is a language of delicacy. You can't just throw half-digested phrases together in a jumble. Go away, come back and start again.
Gila So what I should say?
Mike They "hate" my guts. Anyway, they've probably got no opinion at all about your guts.
Gila So why they don't talk to me? Because you don't teach me the English good, that's why!
Mike Nonsense.

Gila gets up and moves away from the table

Gila Okay, so keep on laughing about me.

Mike gets up, goes to her and puts his arms round her

Mike I'm not laughing about you. Honestly.
Gila I don't want to learn this language no more. I never be able to do more than mumble it.
Mike You're doing very well. It's a thousand times better than it was a month ago. (*He kisses her neck*)
Gila You have everything ready for tomorrow?
Mike I just have to pack my haversack. (*He kisses her neck*)

She turns to him but he goes on kissing her as she tries to speak

Gila Listen, I talk with Ami.
Mike No!
Gila Yes.
Mike Really? How interesting.
Gila Listen to me.
Mike I am.
Gila Give attention to me, Mike.

He tickles her

Stop it. (*She holds his hands to stop him*) I talk with Ami. He say that if we want, we can have house together in the Ghetto. We can have furniture. Nothing special, but some things.

Mike is no longer looking at her

The Ghetto is really for long-stay volunteers only. It would not be right to take house unless you can say for sure that you plan to stay here. Not for ever, of course, but for six months. At least.

She lifts his head so that their eyes meet

Maybe three's okay. (*Pause*) So what you say? You want?

Mike I don't know. I'll think about it.

Gila Make decision now, please.

Mike I can't.

Gila You can.

Mike When we get back from Sinai.

Gila Now. Do it now. Please, Mike. It's not fair for me.

Mike I can't decide now.

Gila Why? (*Pause*) Why, Mike? Because you are thinking you might leave here and go home to England.

Mike No. Not that.

Mike goes back and sits at the table. Pause

Gila Okay, so you must decide one way or the other when we's come back from Sinai! (*Pause*) Okay. (*Pause*) And I just tell you this. I don't intend to sleep no more in this stupid, bloody bed of yours. It's too small for two people. I don't like it. It's having a stupid, bloody . . . (*she mimes a dip*) . . . in the middle.

Mike Dip.

Gila Okay, so "dip"! Stupid, bloody word! I don't sleep in it no more! This is fact!

Mike Come and sit down.

She goes to him, sits on his knee and hugs him close

Gila Oh, Mike . . . (*Pause*) You's telling your Mamma you's lying down with nice Jewish girl?

Mike No.

Gila (*quickly*) She anti-semitic?

Mike No. (*Pause*) What's the matter?

Gila Nothing. It doesn't amount to nothing.

Pause

Mike What? (*Pause*) What? Okay.

Gila Well, I don't know if it's being a good idea for us going to Sinai.

Mike Why?

Gila I don't know. Perhaps it's better if we don't go.

Mike I want to go.

Gila You tell me so little, it makes me sad.

Mike What do you want to know?

Gila Oh, come on, don't treat me like I have wood for brain. For all I'm knowing, you may have wife in England.

Mike Don't be ridiculous.

Gila How am I to know? I must believe what you speak me.

Mike Tell me.

Gila Okay, tell me. Mike on kibbutz is Mike but in England he may be someone else.

Mike eases her off his knee and moves to the other chair. She sits on the chair next to him

Mike I'm worried.

Gila About what?

Mike About what I say to my parents. It's been four weeks and I haven't written a line. They probably think I'm still in Cambridge.

Gila So tell them.

Mike Tell them what?

Gila The truth of why you leave.

Mike I don't know. I told you.

Gila But you don't tell me why. You never talk about these thing.

Mike I just walked out.

Gila But what made you do it? Please . . . try to explain to me.

Pause

Mike I don't know. I was just sitting on the grass one day, down by the river. (*Pause*) Everyone else was lying around and I just thought, that's it, I've had enough. And I just walked away, leaving everything—clothes, money, records, books . . .

Gila People?

Mike And I walked. I just kept walking. Walking and walking in the pissing rain. I just walked. Nothing momentous. No dead birds fell from the trees. No portents. I just walked. All the way along Trumpington Road. (*Pause*) I got as far as Grantchester and I thought, sod it, yes, why not? Do it. The heart of England trip. Get in touch with the true essence of England, what it is to be English. Let the village atmosphere seep into your pores. See if you can make contact with it, this magical thing called Englishness. I wanted to see if I could experience it. The place was deserted. I kept walking, past the old mill, right up around the bend to where the council property starts and I thought: oh, shit, council houses, I'm never going to find the spirit of true Englishness there. So I headed back into the village. Looked at all the usual things; the cottages, the old vicarage and so on and, eventually, as always, ended up in the churchyard; the one where Rupert Brooke is always presumed buried. And there's the poem about the clock stopping. And it's all so wonderful and idyllic. And I was scouting around, vaguely aware that, in fact, I'd actually located it. The English idyll. That this essence of Englishness was actually there, in my possession . . . And suddenly I caught sight of this . . . prat. Sailing down the Cam back towards Cambridge in a punt, with his girl doing all the work, while he reclined at the exact angle, trying to play a chord and strum a tune . . . there was this idiot, sailing along, desperately trying to simulate an atmosphere of . . . Christ knows. Some vague recollection of tranquillity from his grandfather's scrapbook. It was all there. The spires in the background, the river, this typical English village and this prat; this arch tit, sailing through the stillness of centuries, absolutely fucking clueless. (*Pause*) I walked out of the village, got to the main road, turned right instead of left and here I am. How do you put that in a letter. (*Pause*) Are you any wiser?

Gila Uh? (*After a pause*) I listen to what you say, you know.

Mike And?

Gila For me, it's difficult, so many words which I don't know.

Mike gets up and moves about restlessly

Mike Exactly. You see?

Gila You're angry with me?

Mike Not with you. I just feel like screaming.

Gila So scream.

Mike I seem to be the only person on this God-forsaken acreage who can at least feign commitment to a set of principles governing the rudimentary rules for the establishment and pursuit of what we English call "a normal conversation". You understand? Oh Christ, why do I bother?

Gila (*going to him*) You don't think I'm worth it.

Mike It isn't that. It's just that I'm reduced to talking in monosyllables. (*He laughs*)

Gila What this?

Mike There's a limit to what I can say to you, d'you see? There's a boundary to the sorts of things we can talk about. It's frustrating.

Gila So teach me English better.

Mike I'll teach you better English. (*He kisses her*)

Gila You want we should go lie down?

Mike We've been lying down all morning.

Gila I have to do my packing.

Mike No.

Gila Mister Mike . . .

They kiss

Carrie enters carrying easel, paints, sketch pad and stool. She is still wearing her sun hat

Carrie Hi-i. Shalom.

Gila Ah, shit.

Carrie (*coming between Gila and Mike*) How are you two, then?

Mike Fine, thanks.

Carrie Soaking up the sun? And why not! Could you just give me a hand? Won't take a sec.

Carrie hands Mike the easel and he sets it up for her

I've just been talking to some of the women. Very interesting. Very interesting. If only one could paint conversations. Would you mind being a little more careful with that, it was rather expensive. Thank you. Isn't it lovely? I could stay here forever. The trouble I had with this on the plane. You'd never believe. Isn't it funny? I never thought I'd like the sun. But then it's different in England, isn't it? Summer always seems to bring out the worst in people. All those couples in the parks being . . . well, lolling around all over the place. (*She goes to her easel*) Oh, I'm spoilt for choice. There are so many good angles.

She puts the painting on the easel and sits down. She then begins measuring various angles with her thumb, generally making a great play of finding the right angle. Meanwhile Gila stares at the painting

Gila (*horrified*) What this?

Carrie It's the trees and shrubbery over there. They're so beautiful; the lovely reds and greens and browns. It's a bit of a sensual feast, you know, Gila, your home.

Gila (*pointing to the shrubbery*) This that?

Carrie I'm just trying to capture the spirit of it. The essence.

Gila You's having no feel for colour.

Carrie Oh, it's only early stages yet. I'm just dabbling; playing with shapes and forms.

Gila You sit here for million year, baby, still you have no feel for colour.

Carrie Oh well, that's telling me, isn't it?

Gila You must love the brush. The brush don't touch your heart.

Carrie (*to Mike*) She's rather forthright, your friend, isn't she?

Mike returns to his chair

Gila This just noise.

Carrie You paint yourself, then?

Gila flicks one of Carrie's corks, then crosses to Mike

Gila Mike, you come to swim?

Mike I'm writing this.

Carrie So when are you two off on your hols, then?

Mike Tomorrow morning.

Carrie You should have a wonderful time. With Gila.

Mike Yes.

Carrie Lucky old you, you won't be involved in the spectacle of national humiliation. But what can you expect from them?

Mike Who's them?

Carrie You know very well who I mean, Michael.

Mike Do I?

Carrie I sometimes wonder if you're any different.

Mike No, I'm no different.

Carrie You're perverse, Michael. You must be.

Mike Oh, Carrie, shut up.

Gila Come, let's swim.

Mike I'm writing.

Gilla No wonder you is having pink ass! Oh God, shalom. Here comes the Brothers Grimm.

Gila exits taking her towel as Pete and Dave enter. Both are wearing swimming trunks. Pete has a towel tied to his head, Arab style, wears sun glasses and has his suntan lotion sticking provocatively out of the front of his swimming trunks. Dave wears a sun hat and is carrying suntan lotion and a towel. Pete crosses to Mike's table, puts his towel on the back of a chair and sits down. Dave throws his towel on the ground and sits on it

Dave Lovely, eh, Mick? The weather?
Mike Yes.
Dave Nice bit of chicken, lunchtime.
Mike Yes.
Dave Be nice if they cooked it. (*Pause*) They do say raw vegetables are good for you. Can't see it myself. Make me feel fucking ill.

Pete looks across at Carrie's painting, then at the view, then back again in disbelief

Pete Hey, Van Gogh, you got the wages?
Carrie I gave them out at lunchtime.
Pete I wasn't around at lunchtime.
Carrie Then you'll have to come to my room this evening, won't you?

Pete grabs his own throat in mock terror

Dave (*to Mike*) Hardly worth it. Bottle of booze and a couple of bog rolls and they're gone. Makes you think, doesn't it? Ooh.
Pete Stomach?
Dave Agony.
Pete Liquid shit?
Dave Don't.
Pete Vomiting?
Dave My arse feels like it's been burgled. I had to sleep sitting upright all night on the lavvo.
Pete Volunteers' Arsehole, mate. Trust you to be the first. Three days, they reckon, to get rid of that.
Dave It's all these bleeding salads.
Pete You know what you need, Dave? A fucking good holiday away from it all.
Dave Piss off. I mean, come on, let's face it. Nobody told me I'd be working in a bleeding factory. Asked me to do the night-shift.
Dave
Pete } *together*) { Fucking cheek
Mike
Dave I wouldn't even do that in England.
Carrie Have you ever thought of getting involved with the life of the kibbutz? Talking to people, seeing a different society at work? That is what volunteering's all about, you know.
Dave Yeh, well, that may interest you. And what's all this about this bleeding show? It's bad enough working for them all day. Now they're trying to get us working for them all bleeding night, as well.
Pete It's just an excuse for a glorified piss-up.
Carrie It's supposed to be a cultural event.
Pete That *is* a cultural event!
Dave They should be entertaining us.

Carrie The point is to give the kibbutzniks some idea of what life is like where we come from.

Dave They wanna see that, they can go there. I didn't come here to be told what to do.

Carrie What *did* you come here for?

Dave What's it got to do with you? (*Pause*) Who wants to sing songs about England? I've just saved eighteen months to get away from the fucking place. (*Pause*) What time is this meeting? I've got things to do.

Carrie Oh. Such as?

Dave Mind your own fucking business.

Carrie Does everything you say have to be so downright disgusting?

Dave Yes, it fucking does.

Pete He'll be here any minute. He's just having a look at the other groups. (*Pause*) Look at them—chalk and cheese. (*He shades his eyes and looks across the "pool" at unseen groups of volunteers from other countries*) On the one hand, the natives. Some of the best looking women in the world. On the other . . . volunteers. That's what I came for—all those wet-eyed, dark-skinned soldier girls with rifles slung over their shoulders. Out of bounds. That's all *we* get. Volunteers. They're enough to put you off sex for life. Most of them are only here 'cos nobody'll fuck them in England or Sweden or wherever. Europe's rejects. And *we're* supposed to fuck 'em! This is what gets me! I want a nice Jewish girl. I've never had one. I want to sample the locals. Not them.

Pete gets up, moves downstage and gazes across the "pool". Dave sits in the chair

Look at them—I wouldn't go near any of them with a *rented* cock. They're supposed to be Swedes. That's not my idea of a Swede. Is that your idea of a Swede? Swedes are supposed to be sexy. I mean, blondes never look as good the morning after, but look at that lot—and it's not even the night before. I mean, how could you? How could you with *any* of them and not feel the old pangs of self-loathing when you get up to go for a piss?

Dave Hold your water. (*Pause*) Really turns *me* on, all that military stuff.

Pete takes the towel off his head and puts it on the table

Pete I'm in desperate need of female comfort. I keep reading fucking books. I mean, what kind of a life is that. (*Pause. To Mike*) We gave 'em this land, you know.

Mike Who?

Pete Us. Gave the Jew boys this strip of land. Balfour. I was reading up on it. It's in that booklet they gave us.

Dave Haven't read that.

Pete Silly cunt.

Dave What?

Pete Not you—Balfour. Problems we caused, eh? All over the world, anywhere you go, we've been there and fucked it up. Great Britain. Great *fucking* Britain. Must say, you've got to hand it to them.

Mike Who?

Pete The Jews. You've got to admire them. I mean only the Jews could come up with an idea like Volunteering. Just think, they get free labour—that's clever. They get people to travel thousands of miles to *give* their free labour —now that's brilliant! Not only that, but they even get them to pay their own fucking air fare—now that's what I call genius! (*He pulls his glasses to the end of his nose and imitates a "music-hall Jew"*) "Now Mr Balfour's been kind enough to give us this strip of land. It's gonna be sand, sand—and more sand! Not much, but it's a start. Now I've been looking at the figures. And to get this place off the ground is gonna take a great deal of work. But we're only a small deal of a people. What we need is labour. What we've got is sand. Now somebody in their right mind is going to work for a handful of sand? Now I've been in the library all morning, trying to figure out how you create labour out of nothing. And I've come up with the following: Surplus Energy. That's the key. Now what group has surplus energy? (*He smiles*) You've got it. The young. The idealistic. The fucking stupid! Now I've been looking at the word 'volunteer'. If only we can find some reason to convince them it's worth paying their own passage, it'll give it shape. And boys, will it be cheaper! Now I've been looking at the word 'sex'. A handful of sand is not an attractive proposition to the young. But a handful of . . . tit? Or a handful of arse? You get the general drift, boys? Now don't get excited, but I think we've hit on something! The only snag is, whose tit? And whose arse? Now I've been looking at our girls. They are the most beautiful in the world, correct me if I'm wrong? Luscious brown bodies; sad, tempting eyes? No fucking way! Not in a month of Sabbaths. Now, if only we can find some way for them to get *it* without getting *us*. (*He paces around, still acting*) Oh, yoy, yoy, I've got it! I've got it! Hoist the flag! (*He finds a chair and stands on it*) THEY CAN ALL FUCK EACH OTHER! It's perfect. Perfect. We'll provide them with some sort of accommodation, all the raw salad they can eat and two green eggs once a day for breakfast. All right, all right—one green egg!"

The sound of someone clapping enthusiastically. It is Gila as she enters

Gila Good, good. This very good.

Pete Oh Christ. Sorry, it was only a joke.

Gila Yeah, sure. You do this for Volunteers' Day. The kibbutzniks, they love this.

Pete Don't be daft. They'd kill me.

Gila Come on, you's think we's having no sense of humour? Do this.

Mike It's good, do it.

Gila How you are seeing us, to us this is good. It's teaching us something.

Dave Yeah, go on, do it. Then we wouldn't have to do anything.

Pete Nah. Don't want to.

Mike You should.

Pete Forget it, okay?

Gila Ah . . .

Pete I mean it, forget it. (*He moves the chair back and sits on the edge of the table*)

Gila (*to Mike*) Come. We must pack.

Mike There's a meeting.
Gila Not for you. We won't be here for Volunteers' Day.
Mike I'd like to stay.
Gila Why? We'll be in Sinai.
Mike I'll come over as soon as it's finished.

Gila storms off

Pete Never screw a woman first thing of a morning, mate. Makes 'em un-bearable the rest of the day. Nothing to look forward to, see.
Dave How would you know? You been reading up on it?
Pete Fuck off.
Carrie Is that all you can think about—sex?
Pete Except when I look at you. Then I think about egg custard.

Carrie collects her things together and turns to Mike

Carrie Michael, can you please tell Ami I'll be in my room?
Mike Sure.

Carrie marches off

Pete hums the "Laurel and Hardy" tune as she goes

Dave She's a nutter, you know.
Mike What makes you say that?
Dave You know that picture she carries around of her boyfriend?
Mike Yes.
Dave Ain't you noticed anything strange about it?
Mike Like what?
Dave Looks very nineteen-forties; the cut of the jacket, the moustache, the greased-back hair? That's 'cos it is. 'Cos that ain't her boyfriend. That's her old man.
Pete Bollocks.
Dave Fucking weird, eh? Straight up. That fat, Australian tart, Grace, told me. She was suspicious, you know, being as how the geezer looked a bit on the old-fashioned side. So she cross-questions her on the sly, sort-of-style, and bob's your uncle, out tumbles this confession about it being her old man. Eh? And she's making out it's her boyfriend. That he's a doctor in Africa and all that palaver. Ask her to have a look next time you see her.
Pete Why don't you leave her alone? She's obviously not well.
Dave She's a pain in the neck.

The Swedish group can be heard rehearsing a beautiful song

Dave Listen to that. (*Shouting*) Shut up, you bastards. Swedish cunts.
Pete Leave off. I like it.
Dave Balls. (*He sings*)
              "Land of hope and glo-o-o-ory
               Marching off to-oo war . . ."
       (*He begins another song, the tunes getting confused*)
              "There'll always be an Eng-land
               While there are country lanes . . ."

Pete You're a cunt. That's nice.

Dave Fucking rubbish.

Mike At least they've got something.

Dave Ah, crap. What's it all for, anyway?

Pete The kibbutz is what you call an enclosed society. It has to have stuff coming in from outside.

Dave Ooh, listen to him.

Pete Otherwise, it'd stagnate. It's a way for them to see how the rest of the world lives.

Dave Yeah—and only the bleeding Jew boys could come up with a system whereby you don't have to travel to see the rest of the world, the rest of the world fucking comes to you. Hey . . . (*He looks across the* "*swimming-pool*" *and begins to sing again, this time louder*)

> "The German officers crossed the line, taboo, taboo,
> The German officers crossed the line, taboo, taboo,
> The German officers crossed the line,
> They shagged the women and drank the wine,
> Taboo, tabay, ta-bollocky-aye,
> Ta-bollocky-aye, taboo . . .

Dave gets up and goes to the "*pool's*" *edge and motions Pete to join in. Mike looks embarassed. Pete goes to Dave*

> They tied her legs to the end of a bed, taboo, taboo . . ."

Pete joins in, tentatively at first

Pete   "They tied her legs to the end of a bed, taboo, taboo,
Dave   They tied her legs to the end of a bed,
> Shagged her till she was nearly dead,
> Taboo, tabay, ta-bollocky-aye,
> Ta-bollocky-aye, taboo.

(*The pace quickens*)

> They took her down a leafy lane, taboo, taboo,
> They took her down a leafy lane, taboo, taboo,
> They took her down a leafy lane,
> Shagged her back to life again,
> Taboo, tabay, ta-bollocky-aye,
> Ta-bollocky-aye, taboo.
> The German officers went to hell, taboo, taboo,
> The German officers went to hell, taboo, taboo,
> The German officers went to hell,
> They shagged the devil's wife as well,
> Taboo, tabay, ta-bollocky-aye,
> Ta-bollocky-aye, taboo."

The Swedish singing stops

Dave That's fucking shut them up!

Pause. They wander back to the table DR. *Dave sits on the chair and Pete sits on the ground*

I'm bored stiff. (*Pause*) What did you do today?

Pete Got up. Had a shower. Had breakfast. Then another shower. Had a kip. Followed by a shower. Went for a walk. Another shower. Now I'm off again.

Dave Where you going?

Pete For a shit. (*He gets up*)

Ami enters carrying a clipboard and pen. He crosses to them

Dave We was just . . .

Pete Rehearsing.

Ami Go and apologize.

Pete I'll do it. I was on my way, anyway.

Ami When you have apologized, please bring Carrie. Quickly.

Pete Right. Shalom.

Pete exits

Ami looks at his watch

Dave It was only a joke, like. Bit of fun.

Ami (*going to the* CL *table and sitting*) David, why do you sit here all day, waste your life? You never move from the swim-pool.

Dave I like it.

Ami But you never go in the water. If you want I should teach you.

Dave I can swim, honest.

Ami Why don't you visit the library and borrow a book?

Dave Maybe, yeh.

Ami gets up and moves his chair to sit nearer to Dave

Ami David—do you know how many symphonies Mozart write in his life?

Dave Yeh, well . . . Mozart could play the piano.

Ami You should do something useful with your time. You—learn the piano, teach yourself a language, anything, so that when you are leaving kibbutz you are not the same person as when you arrive. You are richer in some way, you understand? Sitting here all day, it's not good for your body or your mind.

Dave I dunno. I get by.

Ami David, what are we going to do with you?

Dave I don't know, Ami, I'm just ignorant.

Ami Oh, David, David—what a precious thing you have in this ignorance. What a gift. To be able to open your eyes and see for the first time—this is not something to be despised. This is the beauty of life. (*Pause*) Do you remember the first time you were in love?

Dave Not really.

Ami I do. I do. I remember the first time I ever see snow. This was England. I see snow for the first time in my life and already I'm twenty-two by then. Such moments of joy can never be repeated. That's where the sadness lies.

You cannot buy them back again for all the money in the world. Enjoy them while you can. Don't throw them away as if they're nothing. Look at you; you're a young man. You're strong. You have a fine back, big shoulders . . .

Dave Knock it off.

Pete and Carrie enter

Ami Twenty-four years of age. Oh, David, I know many young men who would gladly change places with you. Don't waste your life.

Dave Here, Ami, knock it off. I'll be all right, don't worry about it.

Ami Your cynicism is beyond reach. So shalom. (*He puts his chair back*)

Pete goes and leans against shower hut. Carrie moves towards Ami

Okay . . . first, I apologize for being late and second I tell you that Carrie has given up trying to organize your show for Volunteers' Day, so I'm having to do her job as well as my other duties and for this I don't thank you. So, let us go to the culture hall and we check your show.

Nobody moves. Silence

Pete We er—we haven't been able to get anything together.

Ami But you were asked to prepare something. What have you been doing for the past three weeks?

No reply

You see what the Swiss are doing? And the Swedes? They dance around the maypole and sing traditional songs. What about you?

Pete We don't have anything like that. We're English.

Dave See, the problem with this group, Ami, is that we don't have much in common, really.

Ami Well you must work together until you find it. We invite you to live our way of life. You must try. Now Carrie tells me she has given you some poetry to read?

Dave Yeh, well . . . we can't do it.

Ami Why?

Dave Because it's shit, that's why.

Carrie Oh, listen to him.

Ami Keats is shit?

Dave Means fuck all to me.

Ami Pete . . .

Pete Don't talk to me about England, Ami. It's a shitheap. I wouldn't piss on it if it was on fire.

Ami Pete, do you have to swear so much?

Pete Sorry. You did ask. I mean, far as I'm concerned, I thought I'd heard the last of England when I got on the plane. That's why I got on the plane.

Ami It's just a way for us to get to know you. Who you are, where you are from, what careers you are pursuing . . .

Dave Careers? We're peasants, Ami, this group. Apart from Mick. All the other groups are educated, but this group, we're peasants.

Ami You're on a peasants' kibbutz.

Dave Yeh, but half of you lot have been to university and that. You're educated, like Mick.

Ami So what?

Dave Well once you've had an education, you're no longer a peasant, are you? I mean . . . a peasant's a fucking idiot, isn't he? Yokel. Village idiot sort of style. Someone without any brains.

Ami I'm not without brains, I keep telling you this!

Dave Yeh, but you're an Israeli peasant, aren't you? You know, a socialist peasant. Not like ours.

Ami We have to do an entertainment. England is also elegance and——

Pete But that's not *our* England. See you can't realize what we're talking about. There are two Englands.

Ami Okay, so there are two Englands. You know how many different countries the kibbutzniks here come from? We come from all over the world and we live together and work together—why shouldn't you?

Mike gets up and seems to be about to leave

Where are you going?

Mike I'm not going to be here.

Carrie Oh, yes, you've made sure of that, haven't you?

Ami Mike, where are you going?

Mike I'm not involved.

Ami Mike, if these are your friends, why do you not want to be with them?

Mike I didn't say that.

Ami The kibbutz is a social place. What are you doing here if you want to be alone?

Mike When I find out, you'll be the first to know.

Gila enters, unnoticed

Ami (*going to Mike*) Mike, we have been having volunteers here for more than twenty years. The attractions of our life are many—you don't have to worry about accommodation, paying bills, buying groceries. We give you everything free. All we ask is that you work with us. The rest is up to you. (*He looks at the group*) You don't get involved, any of you. So what are you doing here?

Mike We're all here for the cure. All here for the treatment.

Ami And what treatment did you expect to find?

Mike That's my business.

Ami Mike, you are on kibbutz. Your business is our business. Come, tell us.

Mike (*trying*) Look, Ami, I . . . Ah, fuck it.

Ami Oh, well done, Mike. Well done. The English response. What an eloquent nation you are. Fuck this, fuck that, fuck you, fuck off. I don't give a fuck, go fuck yourself. Listen to it. The language of kings has ended in the mouth of beggars.

Mike Now listen, Ami . . .

Ami No, you listen to me, Mike. All of you. By tomorrow night you are

having some idea of a show, you are joining in the life of the kibbutz, or you
go. Home! Back to where you belong! We don't want you here!

Ami collects his clipboard and exits

Carrie (*calling after him*) Does that include me, Ami? Ami, am I included in
that? Ami . . .

She runs off after him

Dave Well that's great, that is. Thanks, Mick, you're a real fucking friend.
Pete (*picking up his towel*) There's no way they're gonna give me the boot. No
fucking way. They want a show about England? They can fucking have it!

Pete exits

Dave Where you going? Great, eh? That's really fucking socialist, that is.
Mike Dave . . .
Dave Fucking cat's out the bag now, isn't it?
Mike Dave, shut up.
Dave Showing their true colours now all right. You can't call this socialism.
Apart from everything else, I can't live on salads.
Gila (*meaning Dave*) Listen to this moron.
Dave Socialism is not about ordering people around.
Gila So what is it about?
Dave Eh?
Gila You're going to talk to me about politics? Kiss my ass!
Dave We gave you this fucking land. Just remember that.
Mike (*intervening*) Think before you speak, Dave, just for once.
Dave Screw yourself, Mick. Come on, Gila, we was having a discussion.
Don't chicken out. We're just shit to you lot. This system here, it don't work.
Gila Young man you got no brain.
Dave We're supposed to be talking politics. But when it comes down to it,
you're scared to have an argument 'cos you know what I'm saying is right.
Gila David, you have the political sophistication of a chimpanzee. I can have
more stimulate discussion with cow's ass-hole. Don't offend me no further.
Dave Ah, what's the use? It's always the same with you communists.
Gila Little boy . . .
Dave Little boy. I like that. I'm fucking older than what you are.
Gila Little English *boy*, if you no like kibbutz, go home. Home to the mother
which love you. We can live here without you, believe me.
Dave Cost you a lot more, though.
Gila David, your arrogance is equal only to your stupidity. Now shut up.
Dave Oh yeah, you've got an answer for everything, haven't you? Anyone
dares argue with you, you call them arrogant. That's just what you said to
Carrie last night.
Gila Hers the arrogance of ignorance, yours the arrogance of idiocy.
Dave Yeh, well I don't reckon this place much, I tell you.
Gila So go. (*She turns away and moves towards Mike*)
Dave I've seen enough, I can tell you that. I've seen all I wanna see, mate.

Don't have to live on the bleeding moon to know it ain't made of green cheese.

Gila (*moving to Dave; angrily but quietly at first*) Who founded the State of Israel?

Dave Eh?

Gila When was it founded?

Dave What?

Gila Who was Theodore Herzl? Tell me.

Dave How the fuck should I know?

Gila What is the name of our Prime Minister?

Dave What is this—*Mastermind*?

Gila Who is it?

Dave I don't know!

Gila So what you do in my country? What you do in my home, you ass-hole? (*She hits David's arm*)

Dave All right, take it easy.

Gila You English, you make me want to sick. You come to kibbutz and you take. Take, take. You give nothing. We invite you to our home so you learn our way of life and we learn yours. But with the English what happen? Nothing. All you want is to lie by the swim-pool and play cowboys and indians for piece of ass. You disgusting peoples. You know nothing of my country. You know nothing of my history. You know nothing of my people. So what you do here, you ignorant bastard? (*She is crying*)

Mike Who founded the Labour Party, Dave?

Dave Aw, don't you start.

Mike Tell her the name of one person who was important in the history of the Labour movement.

Dave picks up his towel and prepares to go

Dave You know what you are, Mick?

Dave exits

Gila These peoples, Mike. These peoples.

Mike It doesn't matter.

Gila They's so stupid.

Mike goes to her

They's having nothing between the ear, (*tapping her forehead*) I mean say, this is Formica. And this Dave, he . . .

Mike He didn't mean it.

Gila Oh come on, why you must always make sorry for him all the time?

Mike Because . . .

Gila What? I don't understand.

Mike No, I don't think you could.

Gila So explain to me.

Mike You wouldn't understand.

Gila Ah, don't give me this bullshit. You know what I'm thinking? Maybe you just the same as them. All bloody volunteers bloody sick in the head.

Mike (*moving away*) Let's pack.

Gila In this I inclusive you.
Mike Include.
Gila So, include. What the bloody differ?
Mike Come on.

Mike collects his things from the table

Gila Where you go?
Mike Let's go and pack. I want to get away from this place.
Gila Mike——

Mike exits

Ah, crazy fucking English.

Black-out. During it, an announcement is heard in Hebrew to introduce the English group's contribution to Volunteers' Day

Announcer's Voice Ve'achshav, namshich bevizua haerev lehagish lachem et hakevutza heanglit vehamishatatfim hem Pit veDavid veheim yeshasheu otanu beshir meod meod mefursam mehahistoria ha'Anglit. Shem hashir hu . . . rak rega . . . Tov . . . Mechiot kapaim roashot lePit veDavid. [And now, we shall proceed with the programme, presenting the English team— Pete and David, who will entertain us with a very famous song from English history. The song is . . . just a minute . . . Well . . . Now some applause, please, for Pete and David.]

SCENE 2

The culture hall/dining-room. Evening, a few days later

It is Volunteers' Day and the various groups are presenting their entertainments. The "stage" is lit with festoons and there is the sound of enthusiastic applause

Pete and Dave enter C through the curtains, holding a large Union Jack between them. A spot comes up on them and the applause continues as they sing extracts from "Underneath the Arches" and "Strollin'"

When they finish singing, they turn upstage, drop the flag and their pants, bend over and bare their arses to the audience. The applause stops

Black-out

SCENE 3

The same. Late the following evening

The hall presents the same appearance as it did in Act I, Scene 1, except that the chair DL is now replaced with another table on which there is a duplicator,

*various stacks of printed and unprinted paper, some folded paper and envelopes.
On the table* DR *there is an ashtray, cigarettes and matches, and a ledger and the
table is littered with papers and some pens. The noticeboard has a large worksheet attached to it and the trolley has cups, a tea urn and milk jug*

When the Lights come up Ami is at the table DL *operating the duplicator*

    *Carrie enters, dressed in cool evening wear and carrying a clipboard. She goes
to the table* DR

Carrie Erevtov. [Good-evening.]
Ami Erevtov. [Good-evening.] You have the worklist?

Carrie refers to her list

Carrie Three holiday, five ill, so there are thirty-two working.
Ami Five ill? Benny is ill, Greta is ill. Who else?
Carrie Monica.
Ami Yes, I know this.
Carrie Aussie Robert.
Ami Again?
Carrie Dysentry.
Ami Sick note?
Carrie He said he was too ill to get to see nurse.
Ami Bullshit. Today he went to the beach at Ashquelon, I know this.

When he has run off enough copies, Ami collates them on the front of the "stage"

Carrie Really?
Ami Ask him to come to my room at nine-thirty. Did you find out who stole
your bed?
Carrie No! (*She makes a note on her list, then begins to make notes on the
noticeboard worksheet*)

    Dave enters tentatively DR

Dave Er . . . (*After a pause*) Hi!
Ami Shalom. (*He looks up*) Yes? What can we do for you?
Dave Well. I was just wondering whether I could — er — have the certificate?
If you wouldn't mind, like. You know, something to remember the place
by?

Ami tuts

Ami This is very inconvenient, David. We are working.
Dave I'd be grateful, Ami. (*Pause*) If you haven't changed your mind, like.
Ami No, David. I'm sorry.

David begins to walk away slowly

    Okay. (*He gets up from his work*) I'll get your certificates.
Dave Just the one. Pete don't want his.
Ami I'm sorry, David. I really am very sorry.

    Ami exits UL

Carrie moves to the table DR *and puts the clipboard down. Dave follows her and leans on the table. Pause. Carrie crosses to the table* DL *and starts putting folded papers in envelopes*

Carrie It was a stupid thing to do.

Dave It wasn't even my idea, it was Pete's. Right mess he's landed us in. I didn't even want to do it. I don't like showing my arse at the best of times. Don't mind if I'm on a bus going somewhere, pressing it against the window for a laugh, but not on a stage, in front of two hundred gawping foreigners. I knew they wouldn't see it as a protest. I said to Pete as we put the Union Jack round us: "I've got a funny feeling this is going to go amiss." Trust me. I'm gonna have to stay in a youth hostel in Tel Aviv until I can get a plane home. That's all my money gone. You're group leader, couldn't you have put a word in?

Carrie Well, I . . .

Dave Suppose you're glad to see the arse-end of us like everyone else. Wouldn't mind betting you put the fucking spoke in. (*He moves to Carrie*)

Carrie I did no such thing.

Dave You think you're superior, that's your problem. Think you're fucking lah-di-dah. (*Pause*) Yeh, well, I know you. I know all about you.

Carrie (*slightly nervous*) What do you mean?

Dave (*facing her*) Coming on you're a fucking nurse. You aren't no nurse. Nurses don't faint when they see a bit of blood.

Carrie What?

Dave So what's the score with you? Eh? What d'you say it for? All those lies.

Carrie What lies?

Dave Everything! Everything you fucking say's a lie! You're sick, you. You know that? Fucking sick.

Pete enters DR *and stands just inside the door*

Pete What'd he say?

Dave He won't reconsider, mate. No way. His mind's been poisoned.

Pete What?

Dave This one here. She put the spoke in.

Carrie I never did. That's a downright lie.

Dave She'd say anything, this one. Like all those lies about her boyfriend.

Carrie (*nervously*) What lies?

Pete Leave it out, Dave. Just leave it.

Dave Coming on it's her boyfriend.

Carrie What lies?

Dave With a demob suit on?

Pete Shut up, Dave.

Dave It's your old man, you fucking loony!

Carrie starts crying and turns away from him

Pete (*grabbing Dave*) Shut up, Dave.

Dave (*to Carrie*) You ain't no different from us.

Pete I said keep your mouth shut.

Dave (*to Carrie*) You're shit like the rest of us.

Pete throws Dave to the floor and stands over him

Pete Why can't you shut your mouth, you prat? What's the point of picking
on her? It ain't her fault.
Dave She got us booted off.
Pete You don't believe that, you creep. (*He turns away from him*) Get up.
Get up before I drag you up, you snivelling snot-rag.

Dave gets to his feet

You blame everyone for everything, but there's one person you never
blame and that's your fucking self.
Dave I don't understand you, Pete. She gets us the boot and you have a go
at me. She's not the only one round here's got a screw loose. I'm beginning
to think there are some slates missing off your roof as well.

Pete (*calling after him*) There's no hope for you, Dave. You're too far gone.

Dave exits

Carrie turns to Pete

Carrie Thank you.
Pete He gets on my nerves sometimes.
Carrie I wouldn't want to come between friends.
Pete He'll get over it. Anyhow, I'll see you.

Pete moves towards the door

Carrie You know, don't you?
Pete Know what?
Carrie Oh, come on, you know. I can tell. You know about my having been
in hospital. Who else knows?
Pete I don't know what you're talking about.
Carrie If they find out, they might kick me off too. You're not supposed to
be here without a medical certificate, if you're not a hundred per cent fit.
Pete How did you get your certificate, then?
Carrie My sister's a nurse. She arranged it. D'you know I haven't had a
Valium for three weeks? I knew I'd be fine once I got away. (*Pause*) That's
why . . . your show . . . I know how you feel.
Pete Yeah, well . . . *we* know how *we* feel. *They* haven't got a clue.
Carrie They might, if you explained things.
Pete How can you explain what it's like in Harlow or wherever.

Gila enters DR, *goes to the tea urn and pours some tea*

Pete Gila, what are you doing here?
Gila This is my home.
Pete But I thought you were in Sinai.
Gila This morning, yes. This evening, home.
Pete Did Mick come back with you?
Gila You think I leave him talking with the Bedouin?

Pete Where is he?
Gila In his room.
Pete Great.
Gila No, I don't think so.

Pete runs off DR

(*To Carrie*) And how it's going with you?
Carrie Fine, fine.
Gila (*crossing to Carrie*) You have something wrong with you?
Carrie It's . . . my boyfriend . . . I've broken off our engagement. I've just sent him a letter. It's never easy, is it?
Gila Shit, men. Why do we bother with them? They're such a pain in the ass. And you English I'll never understand. You can't say two words without there being something behind. All this please and thank you bullshit manners. It's for to hide what's in your heart.
Carrie Did you two quarrel, then?
Gila And Mike, shit. He never talk of nothing but England. I don't know it.

Ami enters UL *with the certificate*

Ami (*going to Gila*) Shalom, Gila.
Gila Shalom.
Ami Manishma? [How are you?]

Gila shrugs

Gila Ani ayefa. Ani holechet lishon. [I'm tired. I go to bed.]
Ami Eich haya beSinai? [How was Sinai?]
Gila Leilatov. [Good-night.]
Ami David — where is he?
Carrie He's gone.
Ami Ah! I bring him his certificate. (*He throws it down on the table* DL, *then takes a pile of papers from the "stage" and sits at the table* DR)

Gila puts her cup on the trolley and moves towards the door UL *as if to leave*

Mike enters

Gila stops and looks at Mike

Shalom, Mike. Why are you back so soon?
Mike Actually, I wanted to have a word with you.
Ami So?
Mike It's about Pete and Dave.
Ami Yes? (*He returns to his work*)
Mike Well — do you have to kick them off?
Ami The decision was taken in a meeting of the whole kibbutz. It's over and done with.
Mike Ami . . . they've worked their balls off for you for weeks. You can't simply cast them off. You owe them something.
Ami Mike . . .
Mike You haven't even listened to what they have to say.

Ami We saw what they have to say. That was enough.

Mike Why didn't you agree to meet them?

Ami No more, Mike, please. There's an end.

Gila (*to Mike*) Why do you put in your nose for these people? They're not worth it.

Mike They wanted to state their case. Surely they deserve that at least?

Ami Mike, you don't know anything about this.

Mike They flashed their arses on stage, I know. They've just told me.

Ami Everybody wants them off kibbutz.

Mike You, too?

Ami Mike, kibbutz is not the right place for everybody. Yes, me too.

Mike Why?

Ami There were women and children present. It was not the kind of joke that we appreciate. In your country, perhaps.

Mike You've learned nothing, have you, from having us here?

Ami On the contrary, Mike. Next time, we choose our volunteers more carefully.

Mike But you've learned nothing about *us*. Absolutely nothing.

Ami You *teach* us nothing, Mike.

Mike They were trying. They were trying to tell you something. Why they're here. What they feel about . . .

Gila Mike, it's too late. We're not English. We can't understand when you talk like this.

Mike picks up some papers from the table

Mike All I'm talking about is this. Democracy. Having a say in your own affairs. Taking decisions about your own lives. You discuss everything which affects you. Things don't get done unless they're good for you. It's not like that in England.

Ami You think this is Paradise? (*He lights a cigarette*)

Mike No, but at least you're not just at the receiving end all the time. The decisions are not taken elsewhere by another group of people, whose way of life is different from yours. That's what it's like for us. They think that we're the same as them, only less so. They think we have the same wants, the same needs but that ours are just a little less acute than their own, just a little less urgent. It never occurs to them that we may want something different. If I try to remain what I am, I get accused of having a chip on my shoulder. In England, I can't be what I am with pride; I can't be what I am with dignity. It's read as arrogance or eccentricity. You have to become one of them. That's the price you pay for a bit of self-respect.

Ami Who are these them?

Mike All of them. They decide everything. Where the schools are going to be, what kinds of schools, what they'll teach. They decide where the towns are going to be, what they'll be like. Oh they'll let us build them. They'll let us be the brickies and the hod carriers, we can do the heavy work. But we must know our place and be grateful to benefit from their learning. We've benefited from it for generations. Walk through any area in England today. Shit heaps, built for us by people who know better. Needless to say, they

never live in their model newtowns. No, they take their architectural awards
and run, back to the village, back to the old ways, while we're left to cope
with the new. These are the people who told us for so long that if we just
kept faith, and worked hard, things would get better. These are the ones
who promised the new Jerusalem, generation after generation. (*Pause*) I
think it's time we ditched that one. I think it's time we started thinking for
ourselves.

Gila slips quietly out of the room UL

Ami So why do you tell me this now?

Mike Because if you kick Pete and Dave off, your system fails them, too.
You've told me so many times that people matter here. That the kibbutz is
different because *people* are important. And because I know you believe
that change is possible.

Ami gets to his feet, deep in thought

Ami Carrie, you are Group Leader, what do you think?

Carrie Well . . . I think they should be given a second chance. Definitely.

Pause

Ami I can make a recommendation. It's by no means certain, but . . . Carrie,
ask them to come and see me in my room—(*he looks at his watch*)—in ten
minutes' time.

Carrie Right.

Carrie exits UL

Ami I should have spent more time talking to you all. (*He collects his papers
together*) But I'm still thinking—is kibbutz the right place for you? At this
time. Go back to university. Finish your education.

Mike And then what? The English don't attack, Ami, they assimilate.

Pause

Ami Kibbutz does not exist in England.

Mike No.

Ami So you must find some other way. (*He picks up his papers*) Shalom,
Mike. Sleep well.

Mike Shalom.

Ami exits UL

Mike goes and leans on the table

*Gila enters with his haversack and coat and puts them on the floor. She turns
to him*

What's this? What have you brought those for?

Gila Take them. Go home.

Mike What?

Gila Kibbutz it's no place for you, Mike. It's better that you go now. Don't
unpack.

Mike I can't. I can't just leave you.

Gila You must. You have no reason to be here. You couldn't hide it in Sinai and you can't hide it here. You must go back. Finish your studies. This is not your home. We are not your people.

They embrace

Mike I'm sorry. (*Pause*) God, why does . . . why does it . . .? (*Pause*) You know, it's only since I've been here that I've realized that *I'm* English, too.

Pete and Dave rush in together DR

Dave Fantastic, fantastic. How did you do it?
Pete Carrie's just told us. Amazing.
Dave Thanks, Mick, I really mean it. Thanks a lot.
Pete I can't believe it. What did you say to him?
Dave Who cares, eh? You did it, that's the main thing.
Gila You're staying on kibbutz?
Dave Yeh, great isn't it?

Gila shrugs

(*To Mike*) Mind you, it won't be the same without you, mate, and that's a fact.
Mike What do you mean?
Dave Gila's just told us you're leaving. It's true, isn't it?

Mike looks at Gila

Gila I'll borrow one of the trucks. We can stay the night in Tel Aviv at my parents' apartment.

Gila exits UL

Pete I'll give you my phone number back home.
Dave Yeah, me, too.

Pete and Dave cross to the table. Pete tears off spare paper from Carrie's clipboard and gives Dave a piece and they write their phone numbers. Dave sits down in a chair, writing slowly

Pete This is my Mam and Dad's. (*He takes the paper to Mike*) That's the code, like, for if you're ringing from outside London.

Mike takes the paper. Pause

Come on, bollocks, we've got to go see Ami.
Dave I'm printing it, to make sure he can understand. (*He takes his paper to Mike*) Hope it's clear enough.

Mike takes it and looks at it

Mike Fine.
Dave That's a seven.
Mike Right.
Dave Made it look a bit like a one.
Mike That's okay.

Pete offers his hand and Mike takes it. They embrace

Pete You . . . If you don't get in touch I'll never speak to you again as long as I live.

They break free. Pete moves towards the door DR. *Dave offers his hand and Mike takes it*

Dave Well, tara for now, then. Fucking hell, I hate this. I hate saying goodbye. I know I'll think of all the right things to say . . . when . . .

They embrace and then break free

Have a nice life. (*He shakes Mike's hand*)

Mike turns away from them

Pete (*quietly*) Come on.

Pete and Dave exit DR

Mike goes to the table and puts the phone numbers down. He puts on his coat and slings his haversack over his shoulder, moves to the door UL *then turns to take a last look around the room. He goes back to the table, picks up the phone numbers and puts them in his trouser pocket. He goes to the door* UL, *switches off the wall light and pushes the door open. A light shines into the dining-room from outside the door*

He exits

Pause then the Lights fade to—

BLACK-OUT

FURNITURE AND PROPERTY LIST

ACT I

SCENE 1

Culture Hall/Dining-room

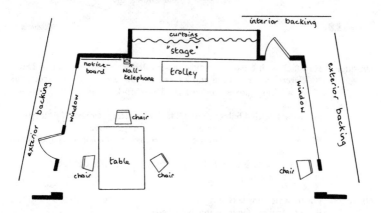

On stage: Table. *On it:* Mike's haversack and suitcase with contents
4 chairs. *Against* DL *chair:* Dave's haversack
Tea trolley. *On it:* tea urn containing tea, cups, jug of milk, tray of sandwiches
Noticeboard. *On it:* notices, posters etc. of kibbutz activities
Wall-telephone
"Stage" curtains closed. *Above curtains:* banner announcing "Volunteers' Day. Thursday 27th."

Off stage: Folding easel, large sketch pad, paints, haversack containing towel, spare pair of shoes **(Carrie)**
Haversack **(Pete)**
Pair of Wellington boots **(Gila)**
Pile of towels **(Ami)**

Personal: **Dave:** pocket comb

Scene 2

Refet (Cowshed)

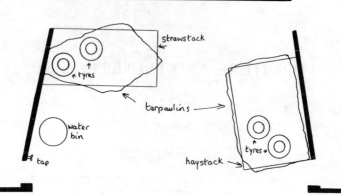

On stage: Haystack with 6 bales practical, assembled with gap behind (for **Dave**).
            Covered by: tarpaulin and 2 tyres. *On top:* 2 pairs of dungarees, pair
            of working gloves. *Against it:* 2 pitchforks, 2 pairs of Wellington
            boots
            Strawstack with 4 bales practical, tied with string. *Covered by:* tarpaulin
            and 2 tyres. *Against it:* pitchfork, broom, 2 shovels
            Water bin with lid containing water. *Hanging from handle:* ladle. *Beside
            it:* toolbox with tools
            Water tap. *Attached to it:* hosepipe tangled with pile of rope
            Hook on DR wall

Off stage: Plastic water bottle **(Gila)**
            Porter's trolley. *On it:* water bin **(Ami)**
            Wheelbarrow **(Mike** and **Gila)**
            Large bundle of string **(Carrie)**
            Large wooden palette **(Ami)**
            Wheelbarrow containing 3 bags of concrete mix **(Mike)**
            Coil of wire **(Ami)**
            Bag of concrete mix **(Gila)**
            Large plastic bucket and rag **(Dave)**
            Bag of concrete mix **(Mike)**
            Trolley **(Carrie)**
            Bike **(Pete)**
            First-aid box **(Gila)**

Personal: **Gila:** watch, milking apron and gloves
            Ami: pocket knife
            Mike: sun hat, orange, postcard in shirt pocket, cigarettes and matches,
                watch

ACT II

SCENE 1

Swimming-pool

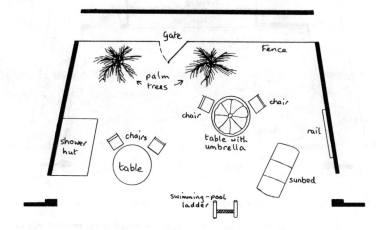

On stage: Garden table C with fixed umbrella open
Garden table DR. *On it:* writing paper, pen (for **Mike**)
4 garden chairs. *On back of* **Mike**'s *chair:* towel
Sunbed. *On it:* towel
Shower hut
2 palm trees
Fence with gate
Swimming-pool ladder (top section only)
Towel rail. *On it:* 2 towels

Off stage: Folding easel, sketch paid with painting, paints, stool **(Carrie)**
Suntan lotion, towel **(Dave)**
Clipboard and pen **(Ami)**

Personal: **Carrie:** sun hat with corks hanging from brim
Gila: towel
Pete: towel, sun glasses, suntan lotion
Dave: sun hat
Ami: watch

SCENE 2

Culture Hall/Dining-room

On stage: "Stage" with curtains closed
Off stage: Union Jack flag **(Pete and Dave)**

SCENE 3

Culture Hall/Dining-room

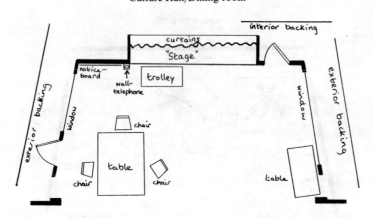

On stage: Table DR. *On it:* ledger, paper, pens, cigarettes and matches, ashtray
                    3 chairs
                Table DL. *On it:* various stacks of papers (printed and unprinted), pile of
                    folded paper, envelopes, duplicator (practical)
                Trolley. *On it:* cups, tea urn containing tea, milk jug
                Noticeboard. *On it:* large worksheet
                Wall-telephone
                "Stage" curtains closed

Off stage: Clipboard and pen **(Carrie)**
                Certificate **(Ami)**
                Mike's haversack and coat **(Gila)**

LIGHTING PLOT

Practical fittings required: festoon lights around "stage" for Act II Scene 2
Various interior and exterior settings

ACT I, Scene 1   Spring dawn
To open: Interior lighting on, dark through windows gradually bringing up daylight

Cue 1   **Gila:** "Oh English — welcome to kibbutz!"   (Page 7)
           Black-out

ACT I, Scene 2   Spring morning
To open: Very bright early morning sunshine

Cue 2   **Mike** and **Ami** exit   (Page 20)
           Quick fade. When ready bring up late afternoon sunshine effect

Cue 3   **Gila:** ". . . your National Health Service."   (Page 28)
           Black-out

ACT II, Scene 1.   Summer late afternoon
To open: Bright sunshine

Cue 4   **Gila:** "Ah, crazy fucking English."   (Page 46)
           Black-out

ACT II, Scene 2   Summer evening
To open: Practicals on

Cue 5   **Pete** and **Dave** enter through curtains c   (Page 46)
           Spot on **Pete** *and* **Dave**

Cue 6   Applause from "audience" stops   (Page 46)
           Black-out

ACT II, Scene 3   Summer late evening
To open: Interior lighting on with interior light outside UL door. Dusk through
               windows gradually fading to night

Cue 7   **Mike** switches off light   (Page 54)
           Snap off interior light in dining-room

Cue 8   **Mike** exits   (Page 54)
           Fade to Black-out

EFFECTS PLOT

Please read the notice on page iv concerning the use of copyright material

ACT I
SCENE 1

Cue 1	To open *Rain effect*	(Page 1)
Cue 2	**Dave:** "He knew it'd get soaked." *Alsatian dog bark in distance*	(Page 1)
Cue 3	**Dave:** "I'm gonna love this place. I can feel it." *Jeep approaching and stopping*	(Page 1)
Cue 4	**Carrie:** ".... the stench of gasolene, doesn't one?" *Alsatian dog bark closer*	(Page 3)
Cue 5	**Ami** disappears quickly. Pause *Telephone rings*	(Page 4)
Cue 6	**Carrie** moves to her haversack *Crop-spraying plane swoops low over the hall*	(Page 5)
Cue 7	**Gila:** "Noise?" *Crop-spraying plane swoops again*	(Page 6)
Cue 8	As Black-out ends SCENE 1 *Radio jingle and programme of American hit records*	(Page 7)

SCENE 2

Cue 9	**Mike:** ". . . turn that up a bit, could you?" *Cut radio*	(Page 8)

ACT II
SCENE 1

Cue 10	**Dave:** ". . . a pain in the neck." *Sound of Swedish group singing*	(Page 39)
Cue 11	As **Pete** and **Dave** finish singing *Swedish singing stops*	(Page 40)
Cue 12	During Black-out at the end of SCENE 1 *Announcement in Hebrew*	(Page 46)

SCENE 2

Cue 13	As SCENE 2 opens *Enthusiastic applause*	(Page 46)
Cue 14	**Pete** and **Dave** drop their pants and bend over *Cut applause*	(Page 46)

SCENE 3

No cues

MADE AND PRINTED IN GREAT BRITAIN BY
LATIMER TREND & COMPANY LTD PLYMOUTH
MADE IN ENGLAND